literature

Literature 5
Teacher Guide

Semester 1

Table of Contents

Classics

Unit 1: Lessons Learned

Introduction

This Teacher Guide contains the main teaching material for the lessons. It includes background information on the important concepts in the lessons, a list of required materials, an activity-by-activity description of what students are learning, and the answers to questions in the lessons.

The Student Pages supplement the Teacher Guide and provide an opportunity for students to work more on their own. While many of the lessons promote independent learning, we recommend that you continue to provide instruction and guidance to your student as necessary. The Table of Contents in this book shows the related page numbers for the Student Pages book in a separate column.

Note that the pages in this book are also available online in the Materials list. The online version should match the book version unless it has an "update" label.

About K12 Language Arts

Introduction

K12's Grade 5 Language Arts program provides a comprehensive sequence of lessons on Language Skills, Literature, and Spelling.

- **Language Skills:** Structured lessons on composition, vocabulary, and grammar, usage, and mechanics.
- **Literature:** Lessons on traditional stories and modern classics, with an emphasis on works that embody exemplary virtues (such as compassion, courage, perseverance, honesty, and loyalty). Lessons are designed to develop comprehension skills, build vocabulary, open the doors to a wide range of imaginative experience, and help your student become a more independent and thoughtful reader.
- **Spelling:** Structured lessons on Spelling. Students develop their understanding of spelling themes and spelling patterns, identify affixes and tell how they affect the meaning of words, and recognize base words and roots in related words.

Getting Started

Lesson Time and Scheduling

- Total lessons: 180
- Lesson time: 120 minutes. Actual lesson time will vary, depending on the individual student. Feel free to split the lessons into smaller segments and provide breaks for your student as needed. K12's online lesson tracking system allows you to pick up wherever you left off on any given lesson.

Grade 5, Course Components and Times

Language Skills	40 min
Literature	60 min
Spelling	20 min

On any given day, a Language Arts lesson includes activities in some, but not all, of the following:

Language Skills	Literature	Spelling
Composition	Classics (including nonfiction)	Spelling
Grammar, Usage, and Mechanics (GUM)	Novels	
Test Readiness	Read Aloud	
Vocabulary	Independent Reading	
	Test Readiness	

Here is a typical week in the Grade 5 Language Arts program:

Minutes	Monday	Tuesday	Wednesday	Thursday	Friday
40	Vocabulary or GUM or Composition or Test Readiness	Vocabulary or GUM or Composition or Test Readiness	Vocabulary or GUM or Composition or Test Readiness	Vocabulary or GUM or Composition or Test Readiness	Vocabulary or GUM or Composition or Test Readiness
60	Classics or Novels or Test Readiness Read Aloud Independent Reading	Classics or Novels or Test Readiness Read Aloud Independent Reading	Classics or Novels or Test Readiness Read Aloud Independent Reading	Classics or Novels or Test Readiness Read Aloud Independent Reading	Classics or Novels or Test Readiness Read Aloud Independent Reading
20	Spelling	Spelling	Spelling	Spelling	Spelling

General Tips
Working Online and Offline

K12's Language Arts program provides a recommended schedule, Teacher Guide, and Student Pages for step-by-step lesson guidance. You will need to print some of these materials, as explained below.

While almost all of the teaching and learning in the Grade 5 Language Arts program is offline, the progress and planning functions and student assessment entry are online.

Please note that some lessons are OPTIONAL. They are provided for students who seek enrichment or extra practice. You may skip these lessons.

If you choose to skip a lesson, then go to the Plan or Lesson Lists online and mark the lesson "Skipped" in order to proceed to the next lesson in the course.

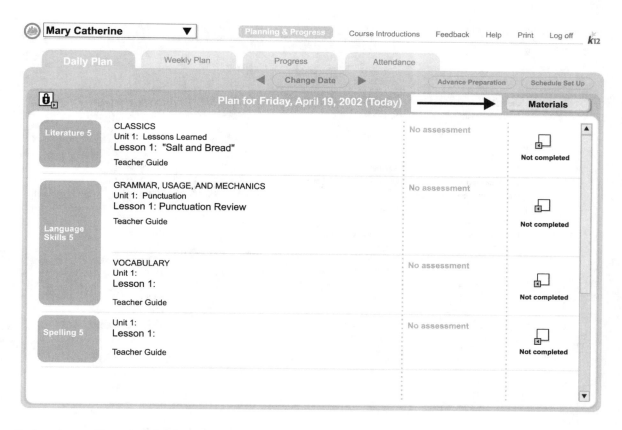

Lessons Supplied in Print

As part of the standard materials for Language Arts, K12 provides paper copies of the Teacher Guide and Student Pages for the lessons which include lessons in Grammar, Usage, and Mechanics; Composition; Vocabulary; Test Readiness; Literature; and Spelling.

K12 also provides *online backup copies* of Language Skills lessons, which you can print as needed from the Materials section of the Planning and Progress area. These online files are provided for your convenience. You do not need to print them, except to replace lost or damaged sheets from the paper lessons you received as part of the standard materials for Language Skills.

If you have trouble accessing any of the websites listed in the Teacher Guide, it is possible that the website has changed. Please go to the online Teacher Guide to get the updated link.

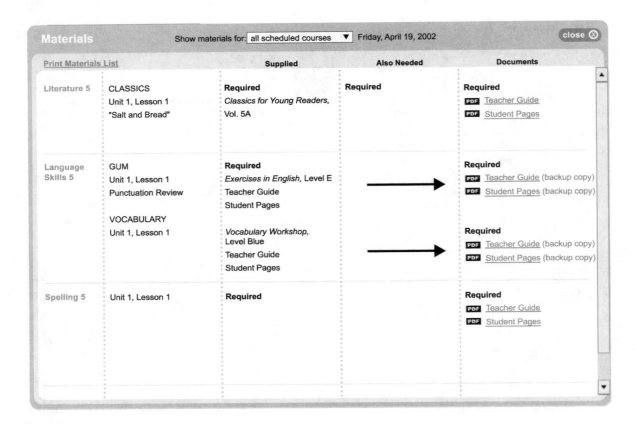

The Portfolio

To record your student's progress in Language Arts, you will need to put together a portfolio. We suggest that you use a three-ring binder with pocket folders to hold:

- Completed practice pages
- Completed lesson assessment pages
- All original compositions, poetry, and artwork

When you complete each unit, take some time with your student to review the Language Arts portfolio and celebrate a job well done!

Safety

Some lessons involve eating or working with food. Before beginning, check with your doctor, if necessary, to assess whether your student will have any allergic reaction to those foods.

Literature Instruction Guide

Lesson Components

K12's Grade 5 Language Arts program provides a comprehensive sequence of lessons on Language Skills, Literature, and Spelling.

The Literature course provides lessons on traditional stories and modern classics, with an emphasis on works that embody exemplary virtues (such as compassion, courage, perseverance, honesty, and loyalty). Lessons are designed to develop comprehension skills, build vocabulary, open the doors to a wide range of imaginative experience, and help your student become a more independent and thoughtful reader.

Grade 5, Course Components and Times

Language Skills	40 min
Literature	**60 min**
Spelling	20 min

Lesson Components and Materials

On any given day, a Literature lesson includes activities in some, but not all, of the following:

Lesson Component	Standard Materials
Classics (including nonfiction)	*Classics for Young Readers,* Volumes 5A and 5B *American Lives and Legends* *Don Quixote* (K12 edition, retold for young readers) *Bard of Avon: The Story of William Shakespeare* by Diane Stanley and Peter Vennema *Paddle-to-the-Sea* by Holling Clancy Holling *American Tall Tales* by Adrien Stoutenburg Nonfiction collections: *Curious Creatures* and *I Didn't Know That!*

Lesson Component	Standard Materials
Novels	N/A
Test Readiness	*Test Ready Plus Reading Longer Passages – Book 5*
Independent Reading	N/A
Read Aloud	N/A

Additional Curriculum Materials

You will need a composition book or three-ring binder with ruled paper to serve as the Reading Notebook in which your student will write responses to questions about the readings. Have your student date each entry in the Reading Notebook and include the name of the story or book used in the lesson.

You will also need to acquire four novels. For more information, please see the section below on Novels.

Classics

Classics lessons include readings in fiction, nonfiction, and poetry, with activities to develop appreciation and skills of literary analysis.

Procedure

Lessons include varying combinations of the following components:

- **Vocabulary:** Defines challenging words in the reading selection.
- **Think Ahead:** Includes questions to review previous reading and prepare for the day's reading.
- **Questions:** Your student writes brief responses to questions in the Reading Notebook, dates the entry, and adds the title of the story or book used in the lesson.
- **Discuss:** You and your student discuss ideas and issues in the readings, in response to questions provided in the lesson.
- **Activities:** Your student completes any of a variety of activities designed to deepen understanding and enhance enjoyment, such as dramatizing part of a story, writing a creative or analytical response, or completing a supplied activity page on comprehension skills (such as describing characters, inferring and drawing conclusions, or comparing and contrasting).

Assessments

Each unit ends with an assessment. Your student completes the assessment on his or her own, and then you check your student's work and enter the results online.

Questions on the unit assessment are similar to those found in many of the lesson activities. The unit assessment allows you to check whether your student is retaining important concepts and skills from the lessons.

To encourage long-term mastery and retention, we provide semester assessments at the midpoint and end of the course. Again, your student completes the assessment on his or her own, and then you check your student's work and enter the results online.

You can use the results of these assessments to guide your review or additional practice. If your student misses any items, we suggest that you go back and briefly review the relevant material in the lessons.

Novels

As part of the Literature course, your student reads four novels, selected from a list of dozens of possible titles designed to meet a variety of interests and reading abilities. You can find these novels at libraries or purchase them at bookstores.

K12 provides lessons for all of these novels. You can access the lessons online, then print them for offline use. More information on the reading level and content of each novel is available in the online lessons.

The novels you may choose from include the following titles. They are listed in order of increasing difficulty as measured by the Lexile scale, a system that measures reading difficulty by sentence length and vocabulary (see www.lexile.com). Lexile ratings roughly correspond to grade levels as indicated below.

Approximate Grade Level	Lexile Range
3	500-700
4	650-850
5	750-950

Keep in mind that because many factors determine an individual child's reading level, it is difficult to rely solely on any numerical rating; thus, these ratings should be used only as a starting point for selecting works of appropriate difficulty.

Novel Choices

Title	Author	Lexile Level
A Lion to Guard Us	Clyde Robert Bulla	360
Stone Fox	John Reynolds Gardiner	550
Sarah, Plain and Tall	Patricia MacLachlan	560
Henry Huggins	Beverly Cleary	670
Charlotte's Web	E.B. White	680
Li Lun: Lad of Courage	Carolyn Treffinger	720
In the Year of the Boar and Jackie Robinson	Bette Bao Lord	730
Little House on the Prairie	Laura Ingalls Wilder	760
The Book of Three	Lloyd Alexander	770
Tuck Everlasting	Natalie Babbitt	770
The Sign of the Beaver	Elizabeth George Speare	770
The Cricket in Times Square	George Selden	780
Mrs. Frisby and the Rats of NIMH	Robert C. O'Brien	790
My Side of the Mountain	Jean Craighead George	810
Call it Courage	Armstrong Sperry	830
Ramona Quimby, Age 8	Beverly Cleary	860
Pippi Longstocking	Astrid Lindgren	870
The Hundred Dresses	Eleanor Estes	870
Shiloh	Phyllis Reynolds Naylor	890
Caddie Woodlawn	Carol Ryrie Brink	890
The Lion, the Witch and the Wardrobe	C.S. Lewis	940
Anne of Green Gables	Lucy Maud Montgomery	990
The Door in the Wall	Marguerite de Angeli	990
Ben and Me	Robert Lawson	1010

Procedure

Lessons may be accessed online and printed for offline use. There are five to ten lessons per novel, depending on the length of the book.

The recommended schedule for Language Arts allots two weeks for the reading of each novel. Your student may take more or less time, as needed.

Lessons include the following components:

- **Vocabulary:** Defines challenging words in the reading selection.
- **Think Ahead:** Includes questions to review previous reading and prepare for the day's reading.
- **Discuss:** You and your student discuss events and ideas in response to questions provided in the lesson.
- **Write:** In the Reading Notebook, your student writes a brief response to questions provided in the lesson.
- **Optional Activities:** Your student may complete any of a variety of activities designed to deepen understanding and enhance enjoyment.

- **Online Review** *(final lesson only):* The final lesson in each unit offers an online review to prepare for the unit assessment. The review, in the form of an interactive game, asks questions about major characters, incidents, and ideas in the novel.

Assessments

Lesson Assessments: Each lesson except the last in a unit ends with an online lesson assessment. Your student should return to the computer to answer questions designed to check comprehension of the reading selection. The results are automatically scored and recorded.

Unit Assessments: The final lesson in the unit presents a Unit Assessment. This assessment is offline, and generally requires that your student write responses to a set of interpretive questions. Your student completes the assessment on his or her own, and then you check your student's work and enter the results online.

Test Readiness

Many of K12's Grade 5 Literature lessons help develop your student's reading comprehension skills. To complement those lessons, we also provide a test preparation booklet from Curriculum Associates called *Test Ready Reading Longer Passages.* This booklet serves a specific practical purpose: the content and format—reading selections followed by multiple-choice questions and a short writing exercise—help prepare your student for similar exercises on many standardized tests.

How the Program Is Organized

- The lessons in *Test Ready Plus Reading Longer Passages* provide practice in answering reading comprehension questions similar to those on standardized tests.
- The test preparation booklet includes reading selections, referred to as passages, from the following genres: Folktales, Narratives, Poetry, Letters, Fables, Informational Text, Biographies, and Point of View Articles.
- The Answer Form, on the back cover of the booklet, lets your student practice recording answers in a "fill-in-the-bubble" format similar to many standardized tests.
- The Practice Test at the back of the booklet gives your student the opportunity to practice answering multiple-choice questions. In the recommended Language Skills schedule, guide your student through this test as his or her first experience with the Test Ready materials.

Independent Reading

This is quiet time for your student to enjoy a favorite book—whatever he or she enjoys most or finds most interesting.

During Independent Reading, try to find a quiet space for your student, free from distractions. If possible, set an example for your student by curling up with a book or magazine of your own. Let your student see that you, too, value and enjoy reading.

In casual conversation, talk with your student about what he or she has read. Share your thoughts about what you have been reading as well. Be a model of enthusiasm and interest in words and ideas.

Your student may devote a section of the Reading Notebook to a log of independent reading. Here, your student can write the title, author, and date that he or she finished reading the work, as well as a few sentences about what your student thought of it.

Read Aloud

Numerous studies have confirmed the value of reading aloud to your student every day. As part of our Grade 5 Language Arts program, we set aside time daily for reading aloud.

Ideas for Reading Aloud

You and your student might have your own favorites for reading aloud. For suggested titles, consult these guides:

- "Children's Classics" recommended by *The Horn Book,* available as a file to download and print at www.hbook.com/parents.shtml.
- *The Read-Aloud Handbook* (4th edition), by Jim Trelease (Penguin, 1995)
- *The New York Times Parent's Guide to the Best Books for Children* by Eden Ross Lipson (Three Rivers Press, 2000)
- *Books That Build Character: A Guide to Teaching Your Child Moral Values Through Stories* by William Kilpatrick, Gregory Wolfe, and Suzanne M. Wolfe (Simon & Schuster, 1994)
- *Great Books for Boys: More Than 600 Books for Boys 2 to 14* by Kathleen Odean (Ballantine, 1998)
- *Great Books for Girls: More Than 600 Books to Inspire Today's Girls and Tomorrow's Women* by Kathleen Odean (Ballantine, 1997)

You might also enjoy reading aloud selections from the following:

- *The Children's Book of America* (Simon & Schuster, 1998); *The Children's Book of Faith* (Doubleday, 2000); *The Children's Book of Heroes* (Simon & Schuster, 1997); *The Children's Book of Virtues* (Simon & Schuster, 1995), all ed. William J. Bennett.
- *Classics to Read Aloud to Your Children* and *Classic Myths to Read Aloud*, both ed. William F. Russell (Crown Publishers, 1992)

Scope and Sequence Literature Grade 5

Comprehension Strategies

- Ask questions and support answers by connecting prior knowledge with information found in, and inferred from, the text.
- Make connections to personal experiences.
- Recall major points in the text and make and modify predictions.
- Summarize readings.

Comprehension Skills

- Recognize the author's purpose.
- Identify the speaker or narrator in a selection.
- Identify and explain cause and effect in literary selections.
- Compare and contrast across selections and genres.
- Make inferences and draw conclusions about characters, supported by evidence from the text.
- Identify the main problem or conflict of the plot and how it is resolved.
- Distinguish between fact and opinion.
- Identify and sequence steps in a process.
- Identify main idea and supporting details of a paragraph or selection.
- Recognize story elements: character, setting, plot (conflict and resolution), theme.

Informational Materials

- Use titles, tables of contents, chapter headings, glossaries, and indexes to locate information in text.
- Follow multiple-step written instructions (e.g., how to use computer commands).
- Locate information in charts, diagrams, maps, captions, illustrations, and photos.

Literary Response

- Recognize different genres: biography, drama, fiction, nonfiction, and poetry.
- Identify and analyze the characteristics of poetry, drama, fiction, and nonfiction.
- Describe characters using examples from the text.

- Describe how a character changes over the course of a story.
- Identify and discuss theme.
- Compare and contrast tales from different cultures.

Poetry

- Identify rhythm, repetition, rhyme, and rhyme scheme.
- Identify and use similes and metaphors.
- Identify and analyze how a poet uses language to appeal to the senses, create imagery, and set tone.
- Identify and discuss theme.
- Recognize literary techniques such as personification, alliteration, and onomatopoeia.

Listening and Speaking Strategies

- Retell, paraphrase, and explain what a speaker has said.
- Read prose and poetry aloud with fluency, rhythm, and expression.
- Connect and relate prior experiences, insights, and ideas to those of a speaker.

Classics

Readings for Classics include the following:

Nonfiction

Two collections:
> *Curious Creatures* and *I Didn't Know That!*

Biography

Bard of Avon: The Story of William Shakespeare by Diane Stanley and Peter Vennema

Historical Fiction

Paddle-to-the-Sea by Holling Clancy Holling

Fiction

A variety of short stories, with an emphasis on traditional tales, organized into the following units:

Lessons Learned
> Salt and Bread
> Ali and the Magic Stew
> The Fire on the Mountain
> The Sword of Damocles
> As Rich As Croesus
> The Three Questions

Poetry

A diverse selection of poems, organized in the following units:

Seasonal Change

"June" by Aileen Fischer

"Summer Rain" by Elizabeth Coatsworth

"That Was Summer" by Marci Ridlon

"The City of Falling Leaves" by Amy Lowell

"The Leaves Do Not Mind At All" by Annette Wynne

"Autumn Woods" by James S. Tippett

"Fall" by Aileen Fischer

"Winter, the Huntsman" by Osbert Sitwell

"Falling Snow" Anonymous

"On a Snowy Day" by Dorothy Aldis

"Snowflakes" by Marchette Chute

"April" by Sara Teasdale

"April" by Eunice Tietjens

"In the Time of Silver Rain" by Langston Hughes

"Spring" by Karla Kuskin

Passing Moments

"The Arrow and the Song" by Henry Wadsworth Longfellow

"Incident" by Countee Cullen

"This Is Just to Say" by William Carlos Williams

"The White Horse" by D. H. Lawrence

"Sidewalk Racer" by Lillian Morrison

"Child on Top of a Greenhouse" by Theodore Roethke

"Base Stealer" by Robert Francis

"Song Form" by LeRoi Jones (Imamu Amiri Baraka)

"The River Is a Piece of Sky" by John Ciardi

"The Tide in the River" by Eleanor Farjeon

"Snow Toward Evening" by Melville Cane

"February Twilight" by Sara Teasdale

"A Bird Came Down the Walk" by Emily Dickinson

"The Eagle" by Alfred, Lord Tennyson

No Matter Where It's Going (poems about travel)

"Travel" by Edna St. Vincent Millay

"A Modern Dragon" by Rowena Bastin Bennett

"Train Song" by Diane Siebert

"From a Railway Carriage" by Robert Louis Stevenson

"Boats" by Rowena Bastin Bennett

"On a Steamer" by Dorothy W. Baruch

"Sea Fever" by John Masefield

"The Airplane" by Rowena Bastin Bennett

"Cockpit in the Clouds" by Dick Dorrance
"Flying" by Kaye Starbird
"Roads Go Ever On and On" by J. R. R. Tolkien
"Roads" by Rachel Field
"The Road Not Taken" by Robert Frost
"The Open Road" by Walt Whitman

American Themes
"Little Puppy"
"The Grass on the Mountain"
"A Song of the Sky Loom"
"A Song of Greatness"
"This Land Is Your Land" by Woody Guthrie
"America" by Samuel Francis Smith
"America the Beautiful" by Katherine Lee Bates
"The Star-Spangled Banner" by Francis Scott Key
"Columbus" by Joaquin Miller
"George Washington" by Rosemary and Stephen Vincent Benet
"Abraham Lincoln" by Mildred Plew Meigs
"O Captain, My Captain" by Walt Whitman
"I Hear America Singing" by Walt Whitman
"I, Too" by Langston Hughes
"The New Colossus" by Emma Lazarus

Novels

Lessons are provided for novels suitable for a range of interests and reading levels, with two novels required per semester. Selections include (but are not limited to):

In the Year of the Boar and Jackie Robinson by Bette Bao Lord
Shiloh by Phyllis Reynolds Naylor
Call It Courage by Armstrong Sperry
The Book of Three by Lloyd Alexander
The Sign of the Beaver by Elizabeth George Speare
Mrs. Frisby and the Rats of NIMH by Robert C. O'Brien
My Side of the Mountain by Jean Craighead George
Caddie Woodlawn by Carol Ryrie Brink
The Lion, the Witch and the Wardrobe by C.S. Lewis
Tuck Everlasting by Natalie Babbitt
Anne of Green Gables by Lucy Maud Montgomery
The Door in the Wall by Marguerite de Angeli
Ben and Me by Robert Lawson

Teacher Guides
and Answer Keys

Classics

Unit 1: Lessons Learned

Identify conflicts within a story and explain how they are resolved. Explore how a character's actions affect the plot of a story.

Lesson 1: "Salt and Bread"

A father learns a lesson about love he will never forget.

Objectives
Demonstrate comprehension of text.
Identify conflict and resolution in a story.

Student Pages
"Salt and Bread"
Characters and Conflicts

Materials
Classics for Young Readers, Vol. 5A, pages 6-8

1. Get Ready

Vocabulary
Go over the vocabulary words with your student before he reads the story.

rumor: (n.) a story, which may or may not be true, that is passed from person to person
It isn't nice to repeat unkind stories that you hear because that is how *rumors* begin.

lavish: (v.) to give or spend in a generous way
The child *lavished* love and attention on her new puppy.

banish: (v.) to force a person to leave his or her country or home as a punishment
"Because you have betrayed me," said the king to the traitor, "I *banish* you from this kingdom forever."

expose: (v.) to make known; reveal
The newspaper reporter *exposed* the truth about the dangerous conditions in the factory.

Think Ahead
Discuss the following with your student.
Have you ever heard the expression, "Listen to your heart"? What do you think this means?

Tip: Talk with your student about how acting on the basis of "listening to your heart"—following the inner promptings of your emotions—is different from acting on the basis of listening to the advice of other people. Sometimes other people tell us to do one thing, but if we "listen to our hearts," we may do something else.

2. Read

Have your student read "Salt and Bread" in *Classics for Young Readers*, Vol. 5A, pages 6-8.

3. Questions

Have your student write the answers to the questions in his Reading Notebook. If he has difficulty, have him read the relevant part of the story aloud.

1. How do the two older girls feel about their youngest sister?
    The two older girls are jealous of their younger sister.

2. Why does the father decide to test his daughters' love for him?
    He begins to believe the lies his older daughters tell him. He doesn't listen to his heart.

3. What does the youngest daughter tell her father about her love for him?
    The youngest daughter tells her father that she values him as salt and bread.

4. What happens when the youngest daughter is sent into the woods?
    The youngest daughter climbs a tree to hide and later meets a young King. They fall in love and marry.

5. What does the youngest daughter leave off the tables at her wedding banquet?
    She leaves salt and bread off the table.

6. What happens to the older daughters at the end of the story?
    At the end of the story, the two older daughters are banished from their father's house.

4. Discuss

Discuss today's reading. If you wish, have your student write a paragraph in response to one of the questions.

1. Why are salt and bread valuable?
    Tip: Discuss how many cultures value salt and bread because they help to sustain life. Some cultures even include bread and salt as part of a wedding ceremony or gift for a new home. Giving salt and bread represents a life that is filled with plenty.

2. What lesson does the father learn at the youngest daughter's wedding?
3. What qualities do you admire in the youngest daughter?

5. Activities

Dear King

Have your student imagine he is an advice columnist for the *Royal Gazette*, a newspaper that serves the local kingdoms in your area. In his Reading Notebook, have him write a paragraph or more in response to the following letter:

Dear Sir or Madam:

I am very upset and not sure what to do. I have three daughters and I love them all. I am certain they all love me, but lately I have been hearing rumors that my youngest child cares very little for me. In my heart, I love her dearly, and I believe she loves me. But I want to test all three children so I can be sure. What do you think?

Yours truly,
An Uncertain King

In his reply, your student should draw on examples from "Salt and Bread."

Tip: Make sure your student understands that the king who wrote the letter has not read the story. But the advice columnist—that is, your student—has read the story, and can use it to give helpful advice to the king who wrote the letter.

Accept any reasonable letter as a response. Look for a response that includes the idea that the king should listen to his heart, or that the king from "Salt and Bread" did not listen to his heart and caused great pain before he learned a valuable lesson about love.

Characters and Conflicts

A *conflict* is a clash or struggle between people, ideas, or feelings. Discuss with your student the different kinds of conflicts in stories. If your student is not familiar with the examples, try to help him think of other stories he knows that illustrate the specific kind of conflict:

A character can have a conflict with:
- Another character or group of characters. For example, Cinderella has a conflict with her stepmother and stepsisters.
- His or her own thoughts and feelings. For example, in the story of "Beauty and the Beast," when the Beast allows Beauty to return to visit her family, Beauty experiences a conflict in her own feelings. Her loyalty to the Beast makes her want to return to him, but her love for her family makes her want to stay with them.
- His or her society or the natural world. For example, in the story of "The Leak in the Dike," the little Dutch boy faces a conflict against the powerful seas that threaten to force their way through the leak.

In a story, characters usually need to *resolve*, or work out their conflicts. Your student knows the meaning of "solve" in "solving problems." Point out how *solve* is hidden in the related word, *resolve*.

Have your student fill in the Characters and Conflicts page with details from "Salt and Bread."

Answers:
1. The two older sisters are jealous of the youngest daughter, and they try to convince their father that she does not love him as they do.
2. At first, the king loves his youngest daughter very dearly.
3. The King experiences a conflict between his feelings of love for his youngest daughter and the uncertainty fostered by the rumors his other daughters have fed him. He listens to others rather than his heart.

4. The conflicts are resolved when the youngest daughter invites her father and sisters to the wedding banquet and leaves salt and bread off the table. This leads the king to understand the tremendous value and importance of salt and bread. When he realizes who his youngest daughter is, he begs her forgiveness, and sends away the scheming older daughters.

Lesson 2: "Ali and the Magic Stew"

In this tale set in old Persia, Ali ibn Ali learns a lesson he will never forget from an unlikely person.

Objectives
Demonstrate comprehension of text.
Identify conflict and resolution in a story.

Student Page
"Ali and the Magic Stew"

Materials
Classics for Young Readers, Vol. 5A, pages 9-16

1. Get Ready

Vocabulary
Go over the vocabulary words with your student before he reads the story.

imperious: (adj.) commanding
The queen spoke with an *imperious* tone when she ordered her page to bring her gown.

audible: (adj.) able to be heard
The speaker's voice was so low that it was barely *audible* to the people sitting in the back row.

delicacies: (n.) rare or special foods that are pleasing to eat
Frog's legs, caviar, and snails are a few of the *delicacies* on the restaurant's menu.

belied: (v.) contradicted
The woman climbed the stairs with a grace that *belied* her elderly appearance.

invalid: (n.) someone who is very sick or disabled
We brought flowers and gifts to cheer up the *invalids* in the hospital.

Think Ahead
Discuss the following with your student.
1. Have you ever learned a lesson from someone unexpected? What did you learn and how did that experience change you?
2. This story is set in a country that used to be called Persia. In 1935, Persia became known as Iran. Locate Iran on a map or globe.
3. Have you ever heard the saying, "walk a mile in someone else's shoes"? What does that saying mean to you?
    Tip: Talk with your student about how it is difficult to understand another person's point of view or feelings unless you imagine that person's experiences.

2. Read

Have your student read "Ali and the Magic Stew" in *Classics for Young Readers*, Vol. 5A, pages 9-16.

3. Questions

Have your student write the answers to the questions in his Reading Notebook. If he has difficulty, have him read the relevant part of the story aloud.

1. What does "he was the apricot of his parents' eyes" mean?
    The saying is a variation of "the apple of my eye"; it means that Ali is very dear to his parents.

2. How does Ali's mother say a true Muslim behaves?
    She says, "A true Muslim gives to the poor, the crippled, the homeless, the hungry."

    Tip: Ali and his family are Muslims—that is, they follow the religion of Islam. If your student has studied K12's History program, he might know about Islam. You can use this opportunity to review or introduce these facts:
    *   The prophet Muhammad founded Islam in Arabia in the seventh century. Today Islam is the world's second largest religion, after Christianity.
    *   The holy book of Islam is called the Koran (also spelled Quran).
    *   One of the fundamental beliefs of Islam is care and concern for the needy.

3. What does Ali's father ask for when he is ill?
    Ali's father asks for shula kalambar, a healing stew.

4. What does Ali do to help his father?
    Ali begs for the coins to buy the ingredients for the healing stew.

5. At the end of the story, the beggar tells Ali to keep the cloak. What is the cloak supposed to remind Ali of?
    The cloak is to remind Ali to be kind and caring. Ali's father tells him, "Let it ever be a reminder that the gentle heart brings life and joy." The beggar tells Ali to keep the cloak as "a reminder of the pain unkindness brings."

4. Discuss

Discuss today's reading. If you wish, have your student write a paragraph in response to one of the questions.

1. Describe Ali ibn Ali at the beginning of the story.
2. Why do you think the healing stew needs to be made with ingredients bought with coins begged from the street?
3. What lessons does Ali ibn Ali learn from his experience begging? How might this change him in the future?
4. At the end of the story, the beggar tells Ali, "I am going and I am staying...I am staying and I am going." What do you think this means?
    Tip: As needed, help your student see that while the beggar himself is leaving the gate, the lesson he taught Ali will remain with him for a lifetime.

5. Activity

Thank You, Sir

Your student will imagine that he is Ali and write a letter of thanks to the beggar. To prepare your student for this writing activity, review the various lessons Ali learned in the story—lessons about how he acts and the way he treats others.

Discuss what *humility* and *compassion* mean. Humility is the quality of being humble, not speaking too proudly of yourself or your own accomplishments, talents, or possessions. At the beginning of the story, Ali lacks humility. He thinks a lot of himself, his family, and his fancy house. He is not grateful for what he has, and he judges the beggar harshly. After having to beg for the coins, Ali learns something about humility.

Ask your student for an example that shows Ali has learned humility. For instance, after he has begged the coins and purchased the ingredients, Ali politely asks the cook to prepare the stew.

Compassion is the ability to feel the suffering of others and be moved to help them. Ask your student for an example that shows Ali has learned compassion. Notice, for example, how Ali helps the beggar at the end of the story.

Have your student pretend he is Ali ibn Ali and write a thank-you letter to the beggar in his Reading Notebook. The letter should explain the lessons Ali learned and how he will act differently in the future. Encourage your student to use the terms you have discussed—*humility* and *compassion*—and to add any other lessons he thinks Ali has learned. Be sure that the letter includes details from the story.

Lesson 3: "The Fire on the Mountain"

Explore the conflicts faced by a character in this Ethiopian folktale.

Objectives
Demonstrate comprehension of text.
Identify conflict and resolution in a story.

Materials
Classics for Young Readers, Vol. 5A, pages 17-22

Student Pages
"The Fire on the Mountain"
Arha's Conflicts

1. Get Ready

Vocabulary
Go over the vocabulary words with your student before he reads the story.

accentuate: (v.) to emphasize
Whenever I start to complain, my mother reminds me of a song that says to "*accentuate* the positive."

durra: (n.) grain grown in warm, dry lands
At the time of the harvest, we will pick wheat, corn, and *durra*.

ordeal: (n.) a terribly hard or painful experience
It is an *ordeal* for me to have my teeth drilled by the dentist.

tantalizing: (adj.) desirable and extremely tempting, but out of reach
The neighbors' swimming pool was *tantalizing* on such a hot day, but it was behind a gate and we didn't have permission to use it.

Think Ahead
Discuss the following with your student.

1. Has there ever been a time when you were treated unfairly? How did you feel? How did you react?

2. A folktale is a kind of story that is told and retold from one generation to the next. Often, folktales are not written down, but are part of an oral tradition, which means they are spoken from memory instead of being read from a book. Folktales are part of most cultures, and are often told to share important ideas or lessons. Can you name folktales that you have been told?

3. This folktale is from Ethiopia, a country on the continent of Africa. Locate Ethiopia on a world map or globe.

2. Read

Have your student read "The Fire on the Mountain" in *Classics for Young Readers*, Vol. 5A, pages 17-22.

3. Questions

Have your student write the answers to the questions in his Reading Notebook. If he has difficulty, have him read the relevant part of the story aloud.

1. Who is Arha?

   Arha is the servant of a rich merchant named Haptom.

2. What question does Haptom want answered?

   Haptom wants to know if it is possible for a man to stand on the highest peak of the mountain through an entire night, without blankets or clothing, and not die.

3. What will Arha gain if he wins the bet with Haptom?

   Arha will win ten acres of farmland, a house, and cattle.

   Tip: You may wish to help your student understand the importance of this bet to Arha. For Arha, owning land will mean that he is no longer a servant, but his own master.

4. How does the wise old man help Arha while he is on Mount Sululta?

   The wise old man helps Arha by lighting a fire across the valley so Arha can watch the fire and think of its warmth and of his friend.

5. Why does Haptom think that Arha did not fulfill the conditions of their bet?

   Haptom thinks his servant cheated because Arha watched a fire, even though it was far across the valley.

4. Discuss

Discuss today's reading. If you wish, have your student write a paragraph in response to one of the questions.

1. Why do you think the wise old man's fire helped Arha survive the cold?
2. After the judge rules against Arha, the old man tells his friend not to lose hope. He says, "More wisdom grows wild in the hills than in any city judge." Explain what this means.
3. What lesson do Haptom and the judge learn at the feast?

5. Activities

Arha's Conflicts

Remind your student that a *conflict* is a clash or struggle between people, ideas, or feelings. Review the different kinds of conflicts in stories.

A character can have a conflict with:
- Another character or group of characters
- His or her own thoughts and feelings
- His or her society or the natural world

In a story, characters usually need to *resolve*, or work out, their conflicts.

As necessary, review the conflicts in "Salt and Bread."

Have your student answer the questions on the Arha's Conflicts page. Make sure he supports his answers with details from "The Fire on the Mountain."

Tip: Discuss each question with your student before he writes. This activity is challenging because it is beginning to lead your student to think beyond "what happens" in the story, and instead to understand what happens in terms of the abstract categories often used in the analysis of literature. Help him make the connection between the specific events in the story and the more general ideas of nature and society.

Answers:

1. On Mount Sululta, Arha's great conflict is with the terrible cold. The cold wind almost freezes him and "chill[s] the marrow in his bones." He begins to feel numb and sick.

2. Arha resolves the conflict by staring at the faraway fire. Although the fire is too far away to warm Arha, through it he manages to find the strength of mind and will to overcome the terrible cold.

3. Arha and Haptom have a conflict about the bet. Haptom bet Arha that he could not spend the night on the top of the mountain without food, clothing, or fire. Haptom says that Arha has not fulfilled the conditions of the bet because he watched a faraway fire.

4. Arha is very sad when the judge rules against him. He feels that he is doomed to the life of a servant and it is as if he never went to the top of the mountain.

5. Arha's conflicts are resolved when Hailu holds a feast and demonstrates why Haptom has been unfair and the judge's ruling was wrong. Hailu prepares delicious food but does not serve the guests. When the guests smell the wonderful food and grow hungry, Hailu tells them that they should feel fed by the smells coming from the kitchen, just as Arha was "warmed" by watching a distant fire.

Lesson 4: Summarizing a Story

Practice boiling down a story to its main events in order to write a plot summary.

Objectives
Demonstrate comprehension of text.
Summarize plot.

Materials
Classics for Young Readers, Vol. 5A, pages 6-22

Student Page
Summarizing a Story

1. Get Ready

Think Ahead
Discuss the following with your student.

1. Why do you think folktales like "Salt and Bread" and "The Fire on the Mountain" are retold from one generation to the next? What makes stories like this last?

    Tip: As needed, remind your student that folktales are part of an oral tradition—stories told and retold, passed from one generation to the next by word of mouth before they are ever written down. Such stories last for many reasons: for example, because they are enjoyable, because they pass on traditional beliefs, because they teach lessons that apply regardless of time, because they give us insight into the basic truths of the heart.

2. As needed, help your student recall or refer back to the following three stories in order to review the main lessons learned:
    *   "Salt and Bread"
    *   "Ali and the Magic Stew"
    *   "The Fire on the Mountain"

    Possible answers include:
    "Salt and Bread": The father learns to listen to his heart rather than be swayed by what others tell him.
    "Ali and the Magic Stew": Ali learns to be humble and compassionate.
    "The Fire on the Mountain": Haptom and the judge learn they must be fair when dealing with others.

2. Activity

A Plot Summary
Your student can demonstrate his comprehension of a story if he is able to summarize the plot accurately and concisely.

Ask your student to tell you the definition of *plot*. (The plot is what happens in a story. It is the sequence of events and actions.)

Emphasize that when we summarize the plot of a story, we include only the most important events and actions. Discuss the sample summary of "Cinderella." Ask your student to help you think of details left out of the summary (for example, the coach made from a pumpkin, the struggles of the stepsisters to squeeze their feet into the glass slipper, etc.).

In his Reading Notebook, have your student summarize one of the stories he has read so far in this unit. He will need to go back to the story and think about which are the most important events.

Tip: If your student has difficulty, go through the story with him and discuss which events he should include in the summary. Have him write each main event as an item on a numbered list. Have him skip lines between each number so that he can go back and insert events if he needs to. When he finishes the list, review it with him and see if any items can be crossed off. Once you agree that you have boiled down the story to the main actions, have him turn the list into a plot summary written in paragraph form.

Lesson 5: "The Sword of Damocles"

Explore differing perspectives in the story of Damocles, who learns that the grass isn't always greener on the other side of the fence.

Objectives
Demonstrate comprehension of text.
Compare and contrast characters' perspectives.

Materials
Classics for Young Readers, Vol. 5A, pages 23-24

Student Pages
"The Sword of Damocles"
Comparing Perspectives

1. Get Ready

Vocabulary
Go over the vocabulary words with your student before he reads the story.

dread: (n.) great fear, especially fear that something bad is going to happen
As the roller coaster climbed to the top of the hill, a feeling of *dread* swept over me.

tyrant: (n) a ruler who is cruel or unfair
The cruel and unjust queen was considered a *tyrant* by most of her subjects.

Tip: You might want to point out that the word *lest* in the first paragraph of the story is an old-fashioned way to say "for fear that," as in: The princess began to prepare for the ball many hours in advance, *lest* she should be late.

Think Ahead
Discuss the following with your student.

1. Do you know the saying, "The grass is always greener on the other side of the fence"? What does that saying mean to you? Have you ever felt that someone else's grass was greener than your own?

    Tip: Be sure your student understands the meaning of the saying—people tend to think that someone else's life or situation is better than their own.

2. People sometimes say, "Be careful what you wish for." Think about that saying as you read today's story.

2. Read

Have your student read "The Sword of Damocles" in *Classics for Young Readers*, Vol. 5A, pages 23-24.

3. Questions

Have your student write the answers to the questions in his Reading Notebook. If he has difficulty, have him read the relevant part of the story aloud.

1. Who is Dionysius? What does he live in fear of?
   Dionysius is a king who lives in fear of someone taking his life.

2. At the beginning of the story, how does Damocles feel about Dionysius's life?
   Damocles thinks Dionysius's life is wonderful and full of happiness.

3. What does Dionysius suggest that he and Damocles do?
   Dionysius suggests that Damocles switch places with him.

4. What dangles over Damocles's head? Why is it there?
   A sword held by a single horsehair dangles over Damocles's head. It is there to show him what it feels like to have his life be threatened at every moment.

5. What lesson does Damocles learn?
   Accept any reasonable answer, for example: Damocles learns that Dionysius's life is not as wonderful as he thought it was, and that the rich and powerful king has great cares and worries.

4. Discuss

Discuss today's reading. If you wish, have your student write a paragraph in response to one of the questions.

1. Why do you think Dionysius wants Damocles to see what his life is like by trading places?
2. Why do you think Damocles does not see Dionysius's life for what it really is until they trade places?

5. Activities

A Matter of Perspective

Discuss how our different interests, desires, and experiences can affect our *perspective* on events.

Have your student consider the different perspectives of Dionysius and Damocles. Ask him to consider who has the more accurate vision.

Have your student complete the Comparing Perspectives page. Have him write in the voice of each character.

Sample responses:
   Dionysius: People think my life is wonderful because I live in this beautiful palace and am surrounded by such fine things. They do not know how much I worry about losing it all. I am powerful, but I do not trust anyone for fear that they will kill me and take all I have.

Damocles: That Dionysius has it made! His life is wonderful. He has so many beautiful things and lives in such comfort. With all that power and wealth, the King must not have any worries at all!

Stories and Sayings

Briefly review how these two sayings apply to today's story:

- The grass is always greener on the other side of the fence.
- Be careful what you wish for.

Discuss how today's story lives on in a saying that people still use. When people feel that something bad or dangerous lies ahead, they speak of having "a sword of Damocles" or "a sword hanging over their heads."

Discuss this very brief sample story to illustrate this saying:

Jenny and Maggie both have a piano recital coming up. In one week, they will perform before a large audience. Jenny has been practicing every day. "I can't wait for the recital!" she says to Maggie. But Maggie, who has not been practicing, groans and says, "I can wait—I feel like I have a sword hanging over my head."

Talk with your student about a situation in which a person might use any of the sayings from today's lesson. Have him write in his Reading Notebook a brief story—just a few sentences, like the sample story on Jenny and Maggie—to illustrate his understanding of one of the sayings.

Lesson 6: "As Rich As Croesus"

Examine an important theme in the story of Croesus, who thinks that as the wealthiest man he must be the happiest—but wise Solon thinks otherwise.

Objectives
Demonstrate comprehension of text.
Explain a story's theme, using evidence from the text.

Materials
Classics for Young Readers, Vol. 5A, pages 25-29

Student Pages
"As Rich As Croesus"
Thinking About Theme

1. Get Ready

Vocabulary
Go over the vocabulary words with your student before he reads the story.

> **prosperous:** (adj.) successful
> The *prosperous* business was able to give raises to all of its employees.

> **feeble:** (adj.) weak
> After the surgery, the man was very *feeble* and needed time to recover.

> **splendor:** (n.) magnificent or beautiful appearance
> When the curtain rose, we were impressed by the *splendor* of the scenery and costumes.

Think Ahead
To prepare for thinking about the theme of happiness in today's story, discuss what happiness means. Ask your student to tell three things that happiness means to him.

2. Read

Have your student read "As Rich As Croesus" in *Classics for Young Readers*, Vol. 5A, pages 25-29.

3. Questions

Have your student write the answers to the questions in his Reading Notebook. If he has difficulty, have him read the relevant part of the story aloud.

1. Describe Croesus.
    Croesus is a very wealthy king. He has horses, land, fine clothes, and many beautiful things. He thinks he is "the happiest man in the world."

2. Why does Solon think Tellus was the happiest man?

    Solon says Tellus was the happiest man because Tellus was honest, worked hard to give his children a good education, and died honorably while bravely defending his country.

3. What happens to Croesus's kingdom?

    Cyrus overthrows Croesus's kingdom. Croesus's "city was taken, his beautiful palace burned, his orchards and gardens were destroyed, his treasures were carried away, and he himself was made prisoner."

4. Fill in the blanks: People still say that a very wealthy man is as rich as _____, and that a very wise man is as wise as _____.

    People still say that a very wealthy man is as rich as <u>Croesus</u>, and that a very wise man is as wise as <u>Solon</u>.

4. Discuss

Discuss today's reading. If you wish, have your student write a paragraph in response to one of the questions.

1. Why do Solon's answers make Croesus unhappy?
2. What lesson does Croesus learn?
3. At the end of the story, why does Cyrus let Croesus go free?

5. Activity

Thinking About Theme

Talk with your student about Croesus's and Solon's very different ideas of happiness. On the Thinking About Theme page, have him explain each character's differing views in the voice of the character. Make sure he understands that he is speaking for Croesus at the beginning of the story, before the king has lost his wealth. Also remind him to use details from the story in his answers.

After your student completes the page, have him read aloud his answers to you. Discuss his statement of the theme of the story.

Accept any reasonable answer for the statement of the theme, for example: Happiness does not come from wealth or power but from living a good and useful life.

Lesson 7: "The Three Questions"

Meet a king in search of answers to three important questions. Think about how you would answer the king's questions.

Objective
Demonstrate comprehension of text.

Materials
Classics for Young Readers, Vol. 5A, pages 30-34

Student Page
"The Three Questions"

1. Get Ready

Vocabulary
Go over the vocabulary words with your student before he reads the story.

> **administrators:** (n.) people in charge of directing or managing something
> The office *administrators* trained the new employees to do their jobs well.

> **diverse:** (adj.) unlike one another; different
> The United States is a nation of *diverse* people.

> **hermit:** (n.) a person who lives alone or away from others
> The *hermit* lived in a cabin deep in the forest, far away from any town or village.

> **vengeance:** (n.) the act of punishing or getting back at someone for a wrong or injury that he or she has committed
> After the raiders robbed the village, the captain cried out to his men, "Let us seek *vengeance* upon those who have done such great harm to us!"

> **reconcile:** (v.) to settle differences, to make up after a fight or argument
> The two friends shook hands and were happy to be *reconciled* after their argument.

> **assaulted:** (v.) attacked with force or violence
> The soldiers took up their spears and swords and *assaulted* the castle of their enemy.

Think Ahead
Discuss the following with your student.

1. Leo Tolstoy, a Russian author of novels and short stories, wrote "The Three Questions." He lived from 1828 to 1910. He is most famous for his great novels, including *War and Peace.* Find Russia on a world map or globe.

2. The king in this story wants to know the answers to three important questions. Think about the following questions:
   - Who is the most important person to you?
   - When is the right time to do something?
   - What is the most important thing to do?

2. Read

Have your student read "The Three Questions" in *Classics for Young Readers*, Vol. 5A, pages 30-34.

3. Questions

Have your student write the answers to the questions in his Reading Notebook. If he has difficulty, have him read the relevant part of the story aloud.

1. For what three questions does the king want the answers?
    The three questions the king wants answers to are:
    1) "How can I know the right time for every action?"
    2) "Who are the people most important to me and to whom I ought to give the greatest attention?"
    3) "What is the most important thing to do?"

2. Why does the king decide to look for answers from the hermit?
    The king turns to the hermit for answers because his advisors give him so many different answers, and the hermit is known for his wisdom.

3. What does the king help the hermit do?
    The king helps the hermit dig with a spade.

4. Why does the wounded man ask for forgiveness?
    The wounded man asks for forgiveness because he had planned to kill the king, but the king ended up saving his life.

5. What are the three answers to the king's questions?
    The hermit's answers to the king's questions are: 1) The most important time is *now*. 2) The most important person is the person you are with. 3) The most important thing to do is "to do good to him."

4. Discuss

Discuss today's reading. If you wish, have your student write a paragraph in response to one of the questions.

1. Paraphrase—explain in your own words—the hermit's answers to the king's three questions.

2. Why do you think the hermit doesn't answer the king's questions right away when he is first asked?
    Tip: Guide your student to understand that the king learns more by experiencing the answers than he would be merely being told the answers. The hermit helps him by showing him, rather than just telling him.

3. Were you surprised by the hermit's answers to the king's questions? Do you agree with the answers?

5. Activity

Write a Diary Entry

Ask your student to choose one of the following characters: the king, the hermit, or the wounded man. In his Reading Notebook, have your student write a diary entry explaining the day's events from the perspective of that character. He should explain the lessons learned or taught by the character and use details from the story.

> Tip: The hermit's entry might include an explanation of why the hermit decided to show the king the answers rather than just telling him. The king's entry might include details about the lesson he learned from the hermit as well as the lesson about compassion that he taught the wounded man. The wounded man's entry might explain the lesson he learned from the king about the importance of compassion and the consequences of vengeance.

After your student completes his diary entry, have him read it to you.

Optional: If your student wants to, have him write his own answers to the king's three questions.

Lesson 8: Roll and Write

Reflect on the details, characters, and lessons learned in "The Sword of Damocles," "As Rich As Croesus," and "The Three Questions."

Objective
Demonstrate comprehension of text.

Materials
Classics for Young Readers, Vol. 5A, pages 23-34

Student Page
Roll and Write
Roll and Write activity page

1. Get Ready

Think Ahead
Discuss the following with your student.
You've read about three kings: Dionysius, Croesus, and the king who asks the three questions. Which of these kings seems wisest to you? Why?

2. Activity

Roll and Write
This activity will help prepare your student for the upcoming Unit Assessment.

Have your student use the Roll and Write page to create a "review cube." He should cut the pattern from the page, fold on the lines, and tape the edges together to form a cube, so that each side of the cube asks a different question.

Have your student roll the cube and read the question that lands face up. Have him pick one of the three stories, and then apply the question to that story. (If he wants to roll again to get a different question, that's fine.)

He should write his answer in his Reading Notebook, and use details and examples from the story to support his ideas.

Have him repeat the process until he has answered three different questions, one question on each story.

Lesson 9: Looking Back

Prepare for the upcoming Unit Assessment by reviewing lessons learned and writing about two characters.

Objectives
Demonstrate comprehension of text.
Describe characters, using evidence from the text.

Materials
Classics for Young Readers, Vol. 5A

Student Pages
Looking Back
Moral of the Story
Character Study

1. The Moral of the Story

Your student has probably read or been told fables that end with a "moral of the story." A moral is a lesson that a story teaches. For example, in the fable of the Tortoise and the Hare, the moral of the story is, "Slow and steady wins the race."

Discuss the concept of a moral with your student, and help him recall morals of familiar fables he might have read, such as:

Fable	Moral
The Fox and the Grapes	It is easy to despise what you cannot get.
The Boy Who Cried Wolf	No one believes a liar, even when he speaks the truth.
The Wolf in Sheep's Clothing	Do not trust appearances.

Have your student complete the Moral of the Story page.

Answers:

"Salt and Bread"	Listen to your heart to hear the truth.
"Ali's Magic Stew"	Have compassion and humility.
"The Fire on the Mountain"	Be just when dealing with others.
"The Sword of Damocles"	Be satisfied with your life and do not envy other people.
"As Rich As Croesus"	Do not place your happiness in wealth and power because no one knows what the future may bring.
"The Three Questions"	Treasure the present moment and the people in it.

Tip: Unlike simple childhood fables that end with a neat moral of the story, the stories your student has read in this unit are more complex and sometimes have more than one lesson, or have lessons that are not easy to boil down to a single statement. If your student thinks a story has a moral other than the one supplied on the page, encourage him to explain his preference.

2. Character Study

As needed, briefly discuss with your student that there are many ways to learn about a character in a story: through the author's description, by what the character says and does, or by what others say about the character.

Discuss with your student this passage from "Ali and the Magic Stew":

"Disgusting grapes!" A handful of fruit flew through the air. Ali was sitting cross-legged with Layla, his small black monkey, on his shoulder. "They are fit only for the beggar who fouls our gate!"

Based on the evidence in that passage, what two adjectives would your student choose to describe Ali? (As needed, remind your student that adjectives are describing words. Possible adjectives for Ali at this point in the story include *selfish, rude, hot-tempered,* and *inconsiderate*.) Have your student write down the two adjectives he chooses, then explain to you why he chose them.

Have your student complete the Character Study page. Point out that in some stories the characters change dramatically, and that if your student wishes, he can choose one adjective to describe the character before he changes and another adjective to describe him after he changes. (For example, Ali changes from scornful to compassionate.) Make sure your student uses details from the story to support his choice of adjectives.

Lesson 10: Unit Assessment

Check your student's recall and understanding with the Unit Assessment.

Objectives
Demonstrate comprehension of text.
Describe a character using evidence from the text.

Lesson Notes
Make sure your student understands the directions for the Unit Assessment, then have him complete the assessment on his own. (He should not refer to the *Classics for Young Readers* book while doing the assessment.)

Part 1

Answers:
1. b
2. c
3. d
4. d
5. a
6. b

Part 2

Your student should write at least one paragraph on one of the following prompts.

A. Describe a lesson that one of the characters learns. Identify the lesson and use examples from the story that explain how the character learns this lesson.

OR

B. Many of the characters in these stories experience a conflict. Choose any character and describe the conflict that he experiences, how he resolves it, and what lesson he learns from it. Use examples from the story to support your answer.

Look back to your student's Reading Notebook entries and to his Characters and Conflicts page, Arha's Conflicts page, and Lesson Morals page for examples of the lessons or conflicts he should write about and the kind of evidence he should provide.

Unit 2: Mostly Heroes

Explore literary heroes from around the world and describe their characteristics. Make inferences and draw conclusions based on evidence from the text.

Lesson 1: "The Story of Mulan": Session 1

Courage and compassion distinguish the hero in this story from Chinese folklore. Read the first part of "Mulan," make inferences, and draw conclusions about the characters.

Lesson Notes
This is the first of two sessions on "The Story of Mulan."

Objectives
Demonstrate comprehension of the text.
Make inferences and draw conclusions supported by textual evidence.

Student Page
"The Story of Mulan": Session 1

Materials
Classics for Young Readers, Vol. 5A, pages 36-46
world map or globe

1. Get Ready

Vocabulary
Go over the vocabulary words with your student before she reads the story.

whimper: (v.) to make a low whining or crying sound
The baby foxes began to *whimper* when the mother fox left the den.

flinch: (v.) to suddenly pull away from something in fear or pain
Even though the shark was in a tank, when it swam near us, I *flinched.*

reproach: (n.) disapproval
My mother looked at me with *reproach* when I pulled my sister's braid.

satchel: (n.) a bag with a carrying strap
I put my library books in my *satchel,* put the strap over my shoulder, and walked home.

Think Ahead
Discuss the following with your student.

1. Have you ever heard of Superman, Hercules, William Tell, or Brave Margaret? They are not real people. They are fictional characters. In their stories, each of those characters is a *hero.* What kinds of things do these heroes do? What words describe them?

Discuss any heroes your student knows best. Your student might mention that heroes fight villains, rescue people in distress, face terrible dangers to help others, etc. Words to describe heroes might include *brave, strong, noble, good,* and *loyal.*

2. Today's story is about a hero from China. Find China on a map or globe.

2. Read

Have your student read Chapter 1 of "The Story of Mulan" in *Classics for Young Readers*, Vol. 5A, pages 36-39.

3. Questions

Have your student write the answers to the questions in her Reading Notebook. If she has difficulty, have her read the relevant part of the story aloud.

1. Why does Mulan say her father cannot go to war?
    Mulan says her father is too old to fight.

2. What will happen if no one from Mulan's family goes to war?
    If no one from Mulan's family goes to war, the Emperor will punish the whole family.

3. Write two things Mulan does to get ready to leave.
    Accept any of the following responses: She bought a saddle, she bought a horse, she changed into her father's iron and leather armor, she tied up her hair and put on a helmet.

4. Discuss

Discuss today's reading. If you wish, have your student write a paragraph in response to one of the questions.

1. Do you think Mulan is brave? Why or why not?
2. Mulan does not have to go to war. Why do you think she decides to take her father's place in the army?

5. Activity

Making Inferences

Read and discuss with your student the section on Making Inferences. When we make an inference, or *infer,* we use the words in the story as clues. What a character says, thinks, and does are all clues that help us make inferences. We think about the evidence in the story, and then we draw conclusions based on that evidence.

Discuss the example from "Ali and the Magic Stew." At the end of the story, when Ali puts his arms around the beggar and asks him to stay, we might infer that Ali has become aware of his pride and selfishness, and that he has become more kind and caring.

To help your student understand what it means to make inferences, you might want to discuss another example. Tell her to think back to the story called "Salt and Bread." What can she infer about the father? The story tells us that he loves his youngest daughter "very dearly." We also know that he asks each of his three daughters to tell him how much she loves him. The youngest daughter replies, "I value you as salt and bread." The story says:

> Then he became angry that she cared no more for him than the humblest things on a poor man's table. His anger turned to fury that his youngest daughter, on whom he had lavished so much affection, thought so little of him in return. And he ordered his servants to drive her out of his house.

Explain that even though we know the father loves his youngest daughter "very dearly," he grows furious and drives her out of the house. He never asks what she meant by saying, "I value you as salt and bread." Based on that evidence, we can infer that the father is rash, headstrong, and ill tempered. We might also conclude that he is vain and self-centered, since he seems to need to hear extreme flattery.

Remind your student to look back to "The Story of Mulan" and think about the evidence as she makes inferences to answer these two questions:

1. How do Mulan's parents feel about her decision to take her father's place? What evidence in the story helped you come to this conclusion?
2. After Mulan decides that she will take her father's place, she buys a saddle and a horse, she dresses in disguise, and she rides away without looking back. What do Mulan's actions tell you about her?

Discuss your student's answers.

Lesson 2: "The Story of Mulan": Session 2

Find out what happens to Mulan, and learn more about her by examining what other characters say and think about her.

Lesson Notes
This is the final session on "The Story of Mulan."

Objectives
Demonstrate comprehension of the text.
Make inferences and draw conclusions supported by textual evidence.
Describe the main character.

Student Pages
"The Story of Mulan": Session 2
The Hall of Heroes (Mulan)

Materials
Classics for Young Readers, Vol. 5A, pages 36-46
crayons or colored pencils

1. Get Ready

Vocabulary
Go over the vocabulary words with your student before she reads the story.

cascade: (v.) to fall like water
The blue silk *cascaded* over the edge of the sewing table like a rippling stream.

tresses: (n.) long locks of hair
Rapunzel's long blond *tresses* reached from the high tower window to the ground.

marshal: (v.) to bring together and put in order
After the battle, the general *marshaled* his scattered troops and marched on.

insignia: (n.) the symbol or badge of a group or person
The king's messengers wore the royal *insignia* on their clothes.

indebted: (adj.) owing gratitude to someone else
I am *indebted* to you for taking care of my dog while I was on vacation.

Think Ahead
Discuss the following with your student.
1. Summarize what has happened so far in the story.
    Remind your student to include only the main events when she summarizes.

2. How do you think Mulan feels as she rides away from home? What do you infer from the statement that "she did not look back"?
    Have your student reread the last paragraph of Chapter 1. The story does not say how Mulan feels, but tells us that Mulan "did not look back." Ask your student to use that description—"She

did not look back"—as a clue to infer what Mulan might be feeling. If needed, prompt with questions, such as: Do you think she is looking forward to the battle? Do you think she is too sad to look back?

2. Read

Have your student read Chapters 2 and 3 of "The Story of Mulan" in *Classics for Young Readers*, Vol. 5A, pages 39-46.

3. Questions

Have your student write the answers to the questions in her Reading Notebook. If she has difficulty, have her read the relevant part of the story aloud.

1. What is Mulan's rank in the army?
    Mulan is a general.

2. For how many years does Mulan fight the enemy?
    Mulan fights the enemy for ten years.

3. What does Mulan ask for when the Emperor offers her anything she wants as a reward?
    Mulan says she doesn't need anything.

4. What does the Emperor give her?
    The Emperor gives her his finest horse and an honor guard to accompany her home.

4. Discuss

Discuss today's reading. If you wish, have your student write a paragraph in response to one of the questions.
1. In Chapter 3, Mulan thinks, "I have disgraced my country and myself by lying." Explain why you agree or disagree.
2. Do you think the Emperor knows that Mulan is a woman? What clues in the story make you think so?

5. Activities

How Others See Mulan
Discuss how a reader can learn about a character by examining what other characters say about her and how they respond to her. Have her go back through the story and find evidence to support her answers to the questions that follow.

Tip: Remind your student that in looking to the story for evidence to answer these questions, she is making inferences and drawing conclusions. Point out that the author never explicitly states that Mulan is a skilled warrior, that she is respected by her troops, or that her soldiers are happy to have her as their general. The reader can draw these conclusions about Mulan by examining what other characters say about her and how they respond to her.

1. Is Mulan a skilled warrior? What do the soldiers say about her?

   Yes, Mulan is a skilled warrior. The soldiers say, "That soldier is a tiger. His sword is ten thousand silver claws!"

2. How do you know the soldiers respect Mulan? What do they do after the battle?

   The soldiers respect Mulan because they invite her to eat with them and they make friends with her.

3. Do Mulan's soldiers like having her as their general? What do they do after her speech?

   Yes, the soldiers like having her as their general. Even though they are tired, after her speech, they cheer and get ready to fight again.

The Hall of Heroes

Have your student complete a Hall of Heroes page for each hero in the unit.

Have your student write the character's name on the line provided, and write a paragraph that explains why the character is a hero. Remind her to write as if her reader has not read the story. Have her describe the hero and give two or more examples from the story to support her opinions. If she would like to draw a picture of the hero, encourage her to do so.

Save this page, as it will be used for review and writing activities later in this unit.

Lesson 3: "St. George and the Dragon"

Meet a legendary knight and princess who defeat a dragon and save a city. Make inferences and draw conclusions about characters.

Objectives
Demonstrate comprehension of the text.
Make inferences and draw conclusions supported by textual evidence.
Describe the main characters.

Student Pages
"St. George and the Dragon"
The Hall of Heroes (St. George)
The Hall of Heroes (Princess)

Materials
Classics for Young Readers, Vol. 5A, pages 47-51
crayons or colored pencils
world map or globe

1. Get Ready

Vocabulary
Go over the vocabulary words with your student before she reads the story.

> **desolation:** (n.) ruin, destruction
> The fire cut a wide path of *desolation* through the countryside.

> **girdle:** (n.) a belt or sash
> The lady fastened a *girdle* of green velvet about her waist and tied her handkerchief to it.

> **yon:** (adj.) an old-fashioned word for "yonder," meaning "far away, in the distance"
> "*Yon* fortress," said the knight, pointing to the castle on the hill, "is where we shall feast this evening."

Think Ahead
Discuss the following with your student.

1. Review "Mulan." What does Mulan do that makes her a hero?
    For example, she fought bravely against a powerful enemy; she risked herself for her family and her country.
2. "St. George and the Dragon" is a tale from England. Find England on a map or globe.

Tip: If necessary, explain to your student that "St." is an abbreviation for "Saint."

2. Read

Have your student read "St. George and the Dragon" in *Classics for Young Readers*, Vol. 5A, pages 47-51.

3. Questions

Have your student write the answers to the questions in her Reading Notebook. If she has difficulty, have her read the relevant part of the story aloud.

1. Why does St. George leave his peaceful, happy lands?
    St. George leaves because he wants to help people in trouble.

2. What is the Princess going to do to try to save the city?
    The Princess is going to offer herself to the dragon.

3. What does St. George do to save the city?
    St. George kills the dragon.

4. Discussion

There are *two* heroes in this story: the Princess and St. George. What makes the Princess a hero? What makes St. George a hero? Have your student find examples of each character's heroism in the story. Help her see that both characters are willing to risk their lives for the good of others. St. George leaves his home and goes looking for those in need of his help. The Princess offers herself to the dragon in order to save the people in her father's kingdom.

5. Activity

The Hall of Heroes: St. George and the Princess
Have your student complete a Hall of Heroes page for each character. As necessary, guide her to write each hero's name on the line, write a paragraph that tells why the character is a hero, and, if she wishes, draw a picture. Remind your student to support her opinions with examples of things the character says and does in the story.

Save this page, as it will be used for review and writing activities later in this unit.

Lesson 4: What Is a Hero?

Define the most important qualities of a hero, and write a royal proclamation calling for a hero.

Objectives
Demonstrate comprehension of the text.
Define important qualities of a hero.
Support definitions with examples from the text.

Student Pages
What Is a Hero?
Calling All Heroes
Hall of Heroes pages for Mulan, St. George, and the Princess

1. Get Ready

Think Ahead
Discuss the following with your student.

1. Summarize the plot of each story.
    Remind your student that to summarize means to tell only the most important parts of the story.

2. Reread your Hall of Heroes pages.
    By reviewing these pages, your student will be preparing for the following discussion and writing activity.

2. The Qualities of a Hero

Engage in a discussion and have your student do a prewriting activity to prepare for a writing task in the next part of the lesson.

Discuss Mulan, St. George, and the Princess with your student. The goal of the discussion is to define the most important qualities of a hero. Discuss:

*   What heroic things does he or she do?
*   What makes the hero different from the other characters in the story?
*   Who is the hero trying to help?
*   Why do you think each character is a hero?

Have your student divide a sheet into three columns and write the name of one hero—Mulan, St. George, and the Princess—at the top of each column. Underneath each name, she should list words and phrases that define why this character is a hero. She may use the same word for more than one character. For example, under all three, she might write "brave." Discuss her lists and guide her to pick and write down the three words or phrases that she thinks are the most important qualities of a hero.

You might want to prompt your student with questions like the following:
*   Is Mulan willing to risk her own life to help others? How about St. George and the Princess?

- Does Mulan seek any reward for her service? How about St. George and the Princess?
- Does anyone have to ask Mulan, St. George, or the Princess to help? Or do they take action on their own?

3. A Royal Proclamation

The purpose of this writing activity is to build on the previous discussion and prewriting in order to define the three most important qualities of a hero, and illustrate those qualities with examples from the stories.

Have your student use the Calling All Heroes page to write a royal proclamation. (As needed, tell her that to proclaim is to announce; a proclamation is an official announcement.) She may look back at the stories and her Hall of Heroes pages for ideas and information.

In the first blank, she should fill in her own name—for example, "the most high and mighty Queen Julia."

Each of the three following paragraphs should name one of three important qualities for a hero, which your student listed earlier in the lesson. Follow this model:

Like Mulan, you must be brave. Mulan showed her bravery by . . . .

Make sure your student provides specific details and examples from each story to illustrate each of the three qualities.

When she has finished, go over her writing with her. If needed, prompt her to go back to the stories to find specific examples for each quality of a hero. Then have her check her writing to correct any errors. Encourage her to read her proclamation to family members.

Lesson 5: "The Last of the Dragons"

An unlikely prince and a surprising princess save the last of the dragons in this tale told with tongue firmly in cheek.

Objectives
Demonstrate comprehension of the text.
Contrast expectations of a hero tale with actual events and characters in the story.

Student Pages
"The Last of the Dragons"
Expectations and Surprises

Materials
Classics for Young Readers, Vol. 5A, pages 52-61
crayons or colored pencils

1. Get Ready

Vocabulary
Go over the vocabulary words with your student before she reads the story.

snout: (n.) an animal's nose
The pig wriggled its *snout* in the mud, searching for food.

unbend: (v.) to relax
After a long week at the office, my father looks forward to the weekend, when he can *unbend* and have fun.

presently: (adv.) an old-fashioned expression for "at once" or "very soon"
"Please go ahead without me," said the princess, "for I will join you *presently*."

fencing: (n.; verb *to fence*) a sport in which two athletes fight with long, slender swords
I put on my special face guard and padded jacket to prepare for my *fencing* lesson.

valor: (n.) bravery, courage, firmness in the face of danger
The king praised the knight for his great *valor* in battle.

philosophy: (n.) the study of basic truths, deep ideas, and great questions, such as, "What is truth?"
He read many books of *philosophy* because he wanted to answer the question, "What is the right way to live?"

neglect: (v.) to ignore, to fail to pay attention
Do not *neglect* the chores you have to do today, or you will only add to your duties tomorrow.

triumph: (n.) the joy of victory or success
The soccer team paraded through the town in *triumph* after winning the league finals.

retreat: (v.) to move back away from an enemy, to withdraw from a battle
After hours of fighting, the soldiers were forced to *retreat* into the woods.

gratitude: (n.) a feeling of thankfulness and appreciation
To express their *gratitude* to our coach, the parents all chipped in to buy him a big trophy.

Think Ahead
Discuss the following with your student.

1. How do St. George and the Princess show that they are heroes?
    They are brave, willing to face terrible danger and risk their lives for others.

2. From the story of "St. George and the Dragon," as well as other stories you've read or heard with dragons in them, what would you expect the dragon in today's story to be like?
    In most tales, dragons are fierce, terrible, and destructive creatures.

2. Read

Have your student read "The Last of the Dragons" in *Classics for Young Readers*, Vol. 5A, pages 52-61.

3. Questions

Have your student write the answers to the questions in her Reading Notebook. If she has difficulty, have her read the relevant part of the story aloud.

1. Does the Princess want to be rescued by the Prince?
    No, the Princess doesn't want to be rescued by the Prince.

2. What does the dragon say about fighting for and eating the Princess?
    The dragon doesn't think it would be a fair fight, he doesn't want to fight, and he doesn't want to eat the Princess.

3. What do the Prince and the Princess offer the dragon?
    The Prince and the Princess offer him a biscuit.

4. Why does the dragon cry?
    The dragon cries because no one has ever called him "dear" before.

5. What does the dragon want to drink?
    The dragon wants to drink gasoline.

6. What does the dragon turn into at the end of the story?
    At the end of the story, the dragon turns into the first airplane.

4. Discuss

Discuss today's reading. If you wish, have your student write a paragraph in response to one of the questions.

1. What do people think the dragon is like? What is he really like?
2. The Princess says, "Everything can be tamed by kindness." What do you think that means?
3. What do you think the Princess means when she says, "You can't tame anything, even by kindness, if you're frightened of it"?

5. Activity

Expectations and Surprises

Read and discuss with your student the section on Expectations and Surprises. Discuss what we *expect* in a tale with a prince, a princess, and a dragon—expectations that have been conditioned by traditional fairy tales and hero tales, as represented by the story of "St. George and the Dragon." The humor in "The Last of the Dragons" springs in part from the surprising contrasts between our expectations of a hero tale and the actual events and characters in this particular tale.

As needed, discuss other examples from the story before your student begins working. For example, we might expect the Prince to be strong and bold like St. George, but this Prince likes to study mathematics and philosophy, and is not strong or good at fencing.

Other surprises your student might notice include:

The Princess does not want to be rescued from the dragon.
The Princess thinks princes are very silly boys.
The Princess is the strongest, boldest, most skillful, and most sensible princess in Europe.

The Prince has a car.
The Prince does not want to kill the dragon.

The dragon won't fight. He doesn't want to eat the princess.
The dragon cries and he's friendly.
The dragon asks for gasoline.
The dragon becomes an airplane.

Lesson 6: Turning a Hero Tale on Its Head

Discuss the conventional elements of a traditional hero tale, as represented by "The Story of Mulan" and "St. George and the Dragon." Write a tale, or part of a tale, that, like "The Last of the Dragons," plays with conventions and surprises the reader with something unexpected.

Objectives
Demonstrate comprehension of the text.
Compare and contrast characters.
Rewrite the ending of "St. George and the Dragon."

Student Page
Turning a Hero Tale on Its Head

1. Get Ready

Think Ahead
Review "The Story of Mulan," "St. George and the Dragon," and "The Last of the Dragons." Have your student tell which was her favorite and have her identify events or characters from the story that she particularly enjoyed.

2. Compare and Contrast

"The Story of Mulan" and "St. George and the Dragon" are hero tales. Compare and contrast the hero tales with "The Last of the Dragons." Discuss the following questions. (The questions are designed to help your student see the conventions that a traditional hero tale follows. If you wish, you can extend this discussion of the conventions of traditional hero tales to other relevant books or movies your student might know.)

1. Describe the main character in a hero tale. What is he or she like? What does the hero have to do?
    The hero is brave, strong, and willing to risk his or her own safety for the good of others. The hero has to face some sort of great danger

2. Describe the battle the hero fights. Does it seem like the hero will win?
    The hero has to battle against an enemy that seems much stronger and almost impossible to defeat. It often seems as though the hero will not prevail, but in the end, he or she triumphs against all odds.

3. Who is supposed to be the hero in "The Last of the Dragons"? What is unusual about him?
    The Prince should be the hero, but is a shy and bookish lad, ready to be led by the spirited Princess.

4. Compare the Princess in "St. George and the Dragon" to the Princess in "The Last of the Dragons."
    The Princess in "St. George and the Dragon" is noble, brave, and self-sacrificing. To save the city, she is willing to sacrifice herself to the dragon, though she never thinks of fighting the dragon. In "The Last of the Dragons," the Princess is clever, spirited, strong, bold, a skillful fencer, and ready to "go and kill the dragon and rescue the Prince."

5. How is the dragon in "St. George and the Dragon" different from the dragon in "The Last of the Dragons"?

    In "St. George and the Dragon," the dragon is a fierce, terrible, destructive monster. In "The Last of the Dragons," the dragon is a sensitive, gentle, and playful creature.

6. In "The Last of the Dragons," what do the characters do instead of fighting?

    They talk, resolve their misunderstandings, and become friends.

3. Activity

Turn a Hero Tale on Its Head

Have your student rewrite the ending of "St. George and the Dragon." Discuss the sample and suggestion provided on the student page. As needed, prompt her with questions or suggestions. Focus on what readers expect and how your student can surprise her readers with the unexpected.

Option: Rather than write a story, your student might prefer to tell it in the form of a comic strip.

Lesson 7: "Robin Hood and Allin-a-dale"

Meet the outlaws of Sherwood Forest and their legendary leader, Robin Hood. Compare and contrast Robin Hood and St. George.

Objectives
Demonstrate comprehension of the text.
Compare and contrast characters.

Student Page
"Robin Hood and Allin-a-Dale"

Materials
Classics for Young Readers, Vol. 5A, pages 62-65

1. Get Ready

Vocabulary
Go over the vocabulary word with your student before she reads the story.

> **trip:** (v.) to dance or skip
> The children returned from the circus, and *tripped* merrily down the sidewalk to their homes.

Think Ahead
Discuss the following with your student.

1. Think about the heroes you've read about so far. What do all these heroes have in common?

2. This story comes from England. Which other two stories in this unit also come from England?
   As needed, help your student recall that "St. George and the Dragon" and "The Last of the Dragons" are also stories from England.

2. Read

Have your student read "Robin Hood and Allin-a-Dale" in *Classics for Young Readers*, Vol. 5A, pages 62-65.

3. Questions

Have your student write the answers to the questions in her Reading Notebook. If she has difficulty, have her read the relevant part of the story aloud.

1. Why do the men live in Sherwood Forest?
   They are outlaws, and so have to hide in the forest.

2. Why do the common people call Robin Hood their friend?
   He robs from the rich and gives to the poor. He sends them help.

3. What does Allin-a-Dale promise he will do if Robin saves his bride?

Allin-a-Dale promises to serve Robin Hood (that is, to join Robin's band of daring outlaws).

4.   What does Robin disguise himself as to get into the church?
       Robin disguises himself as a harper.

5.   What happens when Robin Hood blows his horn?
       Twenty-four men with longbows run into the church when Robin Hood blows his horn.

4. Discuss

Discuss today's reading. If you wish, have your student write a paragraph in response to one of the questions.
1.   The story says that the rich old man "went home in a great rage." Do you think he has a right to be angry?
2.   Compare Robin Hood as a hero to St. George. Does Robin Hood do anything that you think St. George would not do?

5. Activities

Robin Hood and St. George
Help your student extend her consideration of Robin Hood as a hero with further comparison of Robin and St. George. Discuss her responses to the questions before she begins writing

1.   How does he spend his time?
       Robin Hood and his men spend their time roaming about among the trees, hunting the king's deer, and robbing rich travelers. St. George travels throughout the countryside looking for people who need his help.

2.   What words does the author use to describe him?
       Robin Hood is described as daring and lawless. He is a friend to the poor and gives all of his men a fair share of anything that is brought to him. St. George is described as noble, kind, and good. No robbers ever dared to trouble the people who lived near his castle.

3.   How does he treat others?
       Robin is always kind to the poor; the common people look on him as their friend. St. George helps anyone in need.

4.   What do his actions tell you about him?
       Ask your student to support her response with examples from the story.

Optional: A Song of Robin Hood
Have your student reread the poem at the end of the story. Then have her write her own song of Robin Hood. The song may be about the whole story or one scene. It does not have to rhyme. When she finishes, have her make a neat copy of her song and illustrate it.

Lesson 8: "Robin Hood and the Golden Arrow"

Read another story about Robin Hood. Write a speech about whether he is or is not a hero.

Objectives
Demonstrate comprehension of the text.
Write a persuasive speech.

Student Pages
"Robin Hood and the Golden Arrow"
The Hall of Heroes (Robin Hood) (optional)

Materials
Classics for Young Readers, Vol. 5A, pages 66-74
crayons or colored pencils

1. Get Ready

Vocabulary
Go over the vocabulary words with your student before she reads the story.

> **thatch:** (n.) plant material, like grasses or straw used for roofing
> The woman laid bundles of *thatch* together to make a roof for her hut.

> **thoroughly:** (adv.) completely
> I was *thoroughly* embarrassed when I got to baseball practice and realized that I'd accidentally put my jersey on inside-out.

Tip: In part 3 of the story, the phrase "sorely vexed" means "very irritated or annoyed."

Think Ahead
Discuss the following with your student.
1. Why do the poor people in England consider Robin Hood their friend?
    Robin Hood is kind to the poor and sends them help.

2. If you've read tales of Robin Hood before, then you might have met a character in today's story—Robin's foe, the Sheriff of Nottingham. What do you know about the Sheriff?

2. Read

Have your student read "Robin Hood and the Golden Arrow" in *Classics for Young Readers*, Vol. 5A, pages 66-74.

3. Questions

Have your student write the answers to the questions in her Reading Notebook. If she has difficulty, have her read the relevant part of the story aloud.

1. Reread the second paragraph of part 1. What does the sheriff's wife worry about most?

The sheriff's wife thinks about how she looks, what she wears, and whether she appears richer and better off than others.

2. What does the sheriff's wife think of the advice the king gives the sheriff?
    She thinks the king has only made fun of the sheriff, and that the sheriff has acted foolishly.

3. Why does the sheriff fail to catch Robin Hood at the archery contest?
    The sheriff decides to look for a group of men who stay close together, but Robin and his men wear different colors and stay apart from each other.

4. Why does Robin Hood want to give the arrow back to the sheriff?
    Robin Hood wants the sheriff to know to whom he gave the arrow.

5. Who are the monks at the end of the story? How do you know?
    The monks are some of Robin Hood's men in disguise. We know because the purse they give the sheriff has the golden arrow with Robin's note, and because one of the monks "flashe[s] a bright smile at the sheriff's wife."

4. Discussion

Discuss today's reading. If you wish, have your student write a paragraph in response to one of the questions.

1. The sheriff thinks of himself as a "great man." Do you think he is? Why?
2. What does Robin Hood mean when he says, "If the proud sheriff had but borrowed a woman's wit to help him, he'd have put me in the deepest dungeon cell by now"?

5. Activities

Debate at the Hall of Heroes

Have your student write and read aloud a speech that explains why Robin Hood should or should not be added to the Hall of Heroes. Her speech should persuade others to agree with her opinion. Have her compare Robin Hood to at least one other hero. Help her find examples in the stories for support.

Optional: Your student may complete a Hall of Heroes page for Robin Hood, or make a "Wanted" poster for him if she is opposed to Robin Hood.

Lesson 9: "The Horse of Power": Session 1

Examine and enjoy the colorful characters in this hero tale from Russia.

Lesson Notes

This is the first of two sessions on "The Horse of Power."

Objectives

Demonstrate comprehension of the text.
Make inferences and draw conclusions supported by textual evidence.
Summarize the first part of the story from the perspective of one of the characters.

Student Page

"The Horse of Power": Session 1

Materials

Classics for Young Readers, Vol. 5A, pages 75-82
crayons or colored pencils

1. Get Ready

Vocabulary

Go over the vocabulary words with your student before she reads the story.

archer: (n.) a man or woman who uses a bow and arrow
The skilled *archer* could shoot an arrow through a leaf from a hundred paces away.

scarcely: (adv.) hardly
My brother used so much hot water for his shower, there was *scarcely* any left for me.

maize: (n.) corn
The chickens pecked at the golden kernels of *maize* the girl scattered on the ground.

flagon: (n.) a large bottle
The servants brought three enormous *flagons* of wine up from the cellar for the king's feast.

Think Ahead

Discuss the following with your student.

1. Look back at the three most important qualities of a hero you selected for "Calling All Heroes." Keep those qualities in mind as you read "The Horse of Power."
2. Today's story is from Russia. Find Russia on a map.
    If needed, help your student find Russia on a map. Explain that long ago in Russia, the ruler of the land was called the *tsar* (zahr)—he is like a king in other countries.

2. Read

Have your student read Chapter 1 of "The Horse of Power" in *Classics for Young Readers*, Vol. 5A, pages 75-82.

3. Questions

Have your student write the answers to the questions in her Reading Notebook. If she has difficulty, have her read the relevant part of the story aloud.

1. Describe the horse of power.
    Accept any reasonable response: The horse of power is a great horse with a broad chest, eyes of fire, and hooves of iron. He is kind, helpful, and wise.

2. What does the horse of power say will happen if the archer picks up the firebird's feather?
    The horse of power says if the archer picks up the feather, he will be sorry and he will know the meaning of fear.

3. Why does the archer pick up the feather, even though the horse warned him not to?
    He thinks the feather will please his master, the Tsar, and that the Tsar will reward him.

4. What does the Tsar say will happen to the archer if he doesn't bring the Princess Vasilissa?
    The Tsar says, "By my sword, your head will no longer sit between your shoulders"—in other words, the Tsar will cut off the archer's head!

4. Discuss

Discuss today's reading. If you wish, have your student write a paragraph in response to one of the questions.

1. Why isn't the Tsar satisfied with what the young man brings him?
2. The horse of power gives this advice: "Do not be frightened yet, and do not weep. The trouble is not now; the trouble lies before you." What do you think he means by that? Do you think it's good advice? Why?

5. Activity

Journal Entry

Have your student pretend she is the horse of power or the young archer. Ask her to write a journal entry in her Reading Notebook that summarizes the story so far. Have her think about the "voice" of the character she chooses. For example, the horse seems calm, patient, and steady, while the archer is more excited and excitable.

If your student has difficulty, ask her to begin with one of the following prompts:

Horse: "Once again my young master has failed to listen to my advice, and once again he is in trouble. It began when he saw a great feather lying in the path..."

Archer: "Woe is me! When will I ever learn to listen to my wise horse of power? Now I am in such trouble! It all began when I saw a feather lying on the ground..."

Lesson 10: "The Horse of Power": Session 2

Read the conclusion of the tale, make inferences based on what characters say, and discuss whether the archer is a hero.

Lesson Notes
This is the final session on "The Horse of Power."

Objectives
Demonstrate comprehension of the text.
Identify characters by matching them with quotations.
Make inferences and draw conclusions supported with textual evidence.

Materials
Classics for Young Readers, Vol. 5A, pages 82-87

Student Page
"The Horse of Power": Session 2

1. Get Ready

Vocabulary
Go over the vocabulary words with your student before she reads the story.

casket: (n.) a small box
I put my best jewelry in the silver *casket* my grandmother gave me.

cauldron: (n.) a large pot
The *cauldron* was so large that the cook could make soup for thirty people in it.

seethe: (v.) to boil
The water in the hot spring *seethed* and steamed.

Think Ahead
Discuss the following with your student.

1. What has happened so far in the story?
   Your student might simply want to reread the Journal Entry she wrote for the previous lesson.

2. Predict what will happen next. Why do you think that will happen?
   Your student has probably already noticed a pattern in the story. If not, guide her to see how the Tsar makes increasingly unreasonable demands on the archer, the archer despairs, but the horse of power helps the archer find a solution.

2. Read

Have your student read Chapter 2 of "The Horse of Power" in *Classics for Young Readers*, Vol. 5A, pages 82-87.

3. Questions

Have your student write the answers to the questions in her Reading Notebook. If she has difficulty, have her read the relevant part of the story aloud.

1. How does the horse of power catch the tsar of all the lobsters?
    The horse of power wanders slowly over to the lobster and then stomps on its tail with his hoof. Tip: Your student might notice that this is very similar to the way in which the horse caught the firebird.

2. What happens when the archer jumps into the boiling water?
    When the archer jumps into the boiling water, he becomes very handsome.

3. What happens when the Tsar jumps into the boiling water?
    When the Tsar jumps into the boiling water, he disappears in a puff of steam.

4. Discuss

Discuss today's reading. If you wish, have your student write a paragraph in response to one of the questions.

1. Who is the villain in this story? Do you think he deserves what happens to him? Why or why not?
2. Do you think the archer gets what he deserves? Why or why not?

5. Activities

What Characters Say

Discuss the directions for the activity. Have your student try to identify the speaker of the quotations without looking back at the story. If she has difficulty, have her refer to the story. Then have her make inferences about the character based on the words the character speaks. If needed, prompt your student with questions such as, "If you heard someone speak these words, what would you think of this person? What kind of person is he? What words would you use to describe him?"

Your student's inferences may vary from those in the possible answers below, but she should be able to explain the connection between what she infers and what the speaker said.

Answers:

1. The words are spoken by the Tsar. They show that he is very greedy—even though the archer has brought him what he asked for (the firebird), he still demands more. They also show that he is cruel and violent—he threatens to behead the archer if he does not succeed. From these words we can infer that the Tsar is a cruel, selfish, unjust tyrant.

2. The words are spoken by the horse of power. He does not panic or get upset. We can infer that he is calm in the face of danger, and that he values self-control and self-discipline ("Do not be frightened yet and do not weep"). We can also infer that he has wisdom and experience—probably he has been in scrapes like this before, and he has a good sense that as bad as things look now for the archer, they are bound to get worse before they get better.

Hero or Not?

Have your student think back to the essay she wrote about what makes a story character a hero. Discuss whether the archer is like the other heroes she has met—Mulan, St. George, and the Princess. Have her find the words the author uses to describe the archer (young, brave, afraid, etc.) Then have her try to find examples in the story that show the archer acting as a hero.

You might discuss with your student the idea that the archer is not *exactly* like Mulan, St. George, or the Princess, but that he is still a hero, though a different kind of hero.

Lesson 11: Unit Assessment

Check your student's recall and understanding with the unit assessment.

Objectives
Identify characters by matching them with quotations.
Make inferences and draw conclusions about characters, supported by evidence from the text.
Identify and explain two important qualities of a hero.

Lesson Notes
Make sure your student understands the directions for the Unit Assessment, and then have her complete the assessment on her own. (She should not refer to the *Classics for Young Readers* book while doing the assessment.)

A. Who Said It?

Answers:
1. b
2. d
3. f
4. a
5. g
6. c
7. e

B. Making Inferences

Your student should write on two of the three passages. Answers will vary, but in her writing she should use specific evidence from the passage to support her inferences and conclusions about each character. Possible points to look for in your student's answers include the following:

a. We can infer that at first Mulan feels some hesitation before the battle begins. When she sees the enemy warriors, she is sensitive to them as fellow human beings. She wonders, "Who are these people?" We can conclude that when the battle begins, Mulan is both fearless and fierce. She rides into battle "without hesitation," and "war sang in her veins."

b. We can infer that St. George is not content to rest in safety. When he sees that the people are all "safe and happy," he thinks, "They need me no more." We can infer that, as a knight, St. George seeks to help others more than he seeks adventure or glory. He wants to go where there is "trouble and fear," or where there is a woman to be rescued, or even "dragons left to be slain." Because he is willing to leave behind safety and face hardships and dangers, we can conclude that St. George is a very brave and compassionate knight.

c. Robin Hood is excited by the thrill of competing in an archery match. Even though he has heard that the Sheriff of Nottingham will award the prize, he does not hesitate to tell his merry men to get ready for the match. When one man warns Robin that the match is a trick, Robin says that is "the speech of a coward." From that, we can infer that Robin is brave and daring, perhaps even reckless, as he says, "Let us go to the match, come what will of it." We can conclude that Robin Hood's desire for glory and love of adventure are greater than his fear of getting caught.

C. What Is a Hero?

Your student should write two paragraphs that identify what she considers two of the most important qualities of a hero, based on the stories she has read in this unit. She should support each quality with an example from one or more of the stories.

Look back to your student's Calling All Heroes and Hall of Heroes pages for examples of the kind of qualities and evidence she should write about.

Unit 3: The Prince and the Pauper

Read prose and dramatic adaptations of Mark Twain's classic tale of mistaken identity, *The Prince and the Pauper*. Describe, make inferences about, and compare and contrast characters, using evidence from the text.

Lesson 1: *The Prince and the Pauper*

Meet Tom Canty, a poor beggar boy with a rich imagination. Use evidence from the text to describe and make inferences about Tom.

Objectives
Demonstrate comprehension of text.
Describe a character using evidence from the text.
Make inferences and draw conclusions based upon textual evidence.

Student Page
The Prince and the Pauper

1. Get Ready

Vocabulary
Go over the vocabulary words with your student before he reads the story.

pauper: (n.) a very poor person
The charity collected food, toys, and clothes for the *paupers*.

long: (v.) to want something very much
She *longed* to be a great violinist, so she made sure to practice every day.

courtly: (adj.) polite, elegant, in the manner of a royal court
The family had such *courtly* manners that people who had dinner at their house felt as if they were dining with a king and a queen in a grand castle.

pampered: (adj.) being given an extreme amount of care and attention
The *pampered* canary had dozens of toys, a golden water dish, and a huge cage with a small tree inside.

fiend: (n.) an evil or wicked person
He was no ordinary bully; he was so mean to the other children that they called him a *fiend*.

rickety: (adj.) not stable, likely to fall down
The table with the cracked leg was so *rickety* that it would collapse if touched.

passion: (n.) a strong love or desire
My neighbor's *passion* is gardening; his yard blazes with colorful flowers, bushes, and trees that he carefully tends every day.

Think Ahead
Discuss the following with your student.

The Prince and the Pauper is a novel written by Mark Twain. This fictional story is set in England in the 1500s, and it begins on the day Edward Tudor, the Prince of Wales, is born. Everyone in the city of London is celebrating because when Prince Edward grows up, he will become the next King of England.

Background on the author and story:
As necessary, tell your student:
- Mark Twain is a pseudonym, or pen name, for the American author Samuel Langhorne Clemens. Clemens lived from 1835-1910. Two of his most famous works are *Tom Sawyer* and *Huckleberry Finn*.
- The first paragraph of the selection refers to "the sixteenth century." Make sure your student understands that "the sixteenth century" refers to the 1500s (just as the seventeenth century refers to the 1600s, and the twentieth century refers to the 1900s). If you wish, ask your student what century we live in today. (twenty-first)
- Twain's story is fictional, but one of the main characters, Edward VI, was a real Tudor king for a very short time. He was born in 1537. The Tudors were the royal family in England from 1485-1603. If you wish, have your student find England on a map.
- The "Prince of Wales" is a title given to the oldest male heir of the reigning British king. Usually, when the king dies, the throne passes to the oldest male heir. In this story, it is assumed that Edward Tudor, Prince of Wales, will grow up to become the next King of England.
- A *farthing* is a coin used long ago in Britain.

2. Read

Have your student read the selection from *The Prince and the Pauper* in *Classics for Young Readers*, Vol. 5A, pages 88-92.

3. Questions

Have your student write the answers to the questions in his Reading Notebook. If he has difficulty, have him read the relevant part of the story aloud.

1. Where and when does the story take place?
   The story takes place in the city of London in the 1500s.

2. Name and describe the two boys who are born on the same day.
   Accept any reasonable response, for example: Tom Canty and Edward Tudor are born on the same day. Tom Canty is a poor beggar. Edward Tudor is the Prince of Wales. When Edward grows up, he will be the King of England.

3. Describe Tom's real life.
   Accept any reasonable response, for example: In Tom's real life, he is poor. He sleeps on dirty straw on the floor and his father and grandmother are mean. Father Andrew teaches him how to read and write and tells him stories about royalty.

4. What does Tom imagine he is?

> Tom imagines that he is a prince. He organizes a royal court where he and friends act out the affairs of the kingdom.

4. Discuss

Discuss today's reading. If you wish, have your student write a paragraph in response to one of the questions.

1. Do you admire Tom? Use examples from the story to explain why or why not.
2. How does Tom feel about his life? What can you infer about him based on these feelings?

5. Activity

Character Study

In this activity, have your student find evidence in the text to show how imagining and reading changed Tom's life.

Remind your student that readers learn about characters by paying attention to what they say and do, and what others say about them. Readers can also make inferences about characters. To make an inference means to think about the evidence in the story and draw conclusions based on that evidence.

First, discuss with your student the following questions:

- What does the priest teach Tom? What kinds of stories does Tom read and hear? (The priest teaches Tom how to read and write, a little Latin, and the right way to act. Tom reads and hears fairy tales and stories about royalty.)
- What does Tom dream about afterwards? (He dreams about being a prince in a castle.)
- How do Tom's behavior and ideas change? What does he think about and wish for? (He begins to see his own life as lacking. He finds his clothes shabby and he wishes to be clean. He begins to act like a prince. He speaks well and has good manners. He plays pretend court with his family and friends.)
- How do other people react to his changes? (The boys are in awe of him. Grown-ups bring their problems to him and he gives them advice. He is everyone's hero except for his own family.)

After your discussion, have your student draw conclusions about Tom Canty. In his Reading Notebook, your student should write a paragraph describing the kind of person Tom is. Remind your student to use evidence from the story to support his ideas.

Lesson 2: "The Prince and the Pauper" (A Play): Session 1

In the first half of this play based on Mark Twain's novel, Tom Canty and the Prince meet, exchange clothes, and are accidentally cast into each other's lives. Identify dramatic conventions, make inferences about the main characters, and rewrite examples of antiquated speech.

Lesson Notes
This is the first of two sessions on "The Prince and the Pauper" (A Play).

Objectives
Demonstrate comprehension of text.
Identify dramatic conventions.
Describe a character, using evidence from the text.
Make inferences and draw conclusions based upon textual evidence.

Student Page
"The Prince and the Pauper" (A Play): Session 1

1. Get Ready

Vocabulary
Go over the vocabulary words with your student before he reads the story.

glimpse: (n.) a quick look
We caught a *glimpse* of the hummingbird as it darted past our window.

indignantly: (adv.) filled with anger because of injustice
When Tommy saw the tiger pacing back and forth in its cage at the zoo, he cried *indignantly*, "They should send that poor animal back to the jungle!"

stature: (n.) height
When he stood up, he rose to such a *stature*, he looked like a giant to me.

differ: (v.) to have different opinions, to disagree
Sometimes my parents and I *differ* about what time I should go to bed.

crave: (v.) to want very much
After two hours in the noisy, busy store, I began to *crave* the peace and quiet of home.

hesitantly: (adv.) not being sure of oneself, holding back
The baby bird crept *hesitantly* to the edge of the nest, spread its wings for the first time, and flew.

etiquette: (n.) correct behavior
It is proper *etiquette* to keep your elbows off the table while eating dinner.

Think Ahead
1. Summarize the chapters from *The Prince and the Pauper*.

    Tip: To prepare your student for the assessment at the end of the unit, make sure he includes the following information in his summary:

- The author's name (Mark Twain)
- The main character's name (Tom Canty)
- What Tom's life is like (Accept any reasonable response, for example: He is a beggar, his father and grandmother are cruel, he sleeps on dirty straw on the floor, the priest teaches him how to do right and tells him stories, he pretends he is a prince.)
- What Tom wishes (Tom wishes he could see a prince and pretends he is royalty)

2. Focus on the conventions of how plays are written on the page. If your student is already familiar with reading scripts, have him read quickly through this section for review. If he is new to reading plays, then use the questions to guide him through reading the first pages of the play. Make sure he understands the following:

- *Dramatized* means that a story has been rewritten as a play.
- The characters in a play are listed before the text of the play begins.
- A play is divided into scenes. (Some plays are divided into acts, which are subdivided into scenes.)
- The script provides stage directions in parentheses. Stage directions tell the actors where to move and how to read certain lines. Stage directions are *not* read aloud.
- This play is unusual in that it has a character called the *Narrator*. The Narrator stands outside the play. He or she explains what is happening and frequently provides additional information about the setting or plot.

Tip: As needed, review that when characters talk to each other in a play, it is called *dialogue*. In a script, there is no need for quotation marks because each speaker is identified in turn. For instance:
PRINCE: Good. Now that I've dismissed my attendants, we can talk. What is your name?
TOM: Tom Canty, if it please you, sir.

If it is difficult for your student to follow the dialogue as it switches from one character to another, suggest that he use an index card as a marker to keep his place on the page as he reads.

2. Read

Have your student read Scenes 1 and 2 of "The Prince and the Pauper" in *Classics for Young Readers*, Vol. 5A, pages 93-101.

3. Questions

Have your student write the answers to the questions in his Reading Notebook. If he has difficulty, have him read the relevant part of the story aloud.

1. How do Tom and Prince Edward meet?
    Tom and Prince Edward meet when Tom goes to see the Prince outside the palace. The palace guards grab Tom and try to remove him. The Prince makes the guards put Tom down and invites him inside.

2. What do the boys decide to do?
    The boys decide to change clothes.

3. What is unusual about the boys' appearances?

      They look alike.

4. What happens to the real Prince?

      He is mistaken for Tom and dragged to the Canty home by Tom's father.

5. What do the members of the court think has happened to their Prince?

      The members of the court think the Prince has gone mad.

4. Discuss

Discuss today's reading. If you wish, have your student write a paragraph in response to one of the questions.

1. Is Tom happy being a prince? Why or why not?
2. Based upon what you have learned about Tom, predict what he will do.

5. Activities

Exploring Language

As necessary, explain to your student that language changes over time. Some words were invented long ago, but aren't used often or at all today, like *methinks*. Old, rarely-used words are called *archaic* words. *Methinks* means "I think."

Sample Answers:
1. He's always liked pretending he's a prince in a court, but now he's gone totally crazy.
2. I think I've forgotten that, too!

Character Study

Briefly discuss with your student that *the way* a character says something can be just as important as *what* the character says. We can make inferences about the kind of person the character is by paying attention to how he speaks.

Have your student read aloud the Prince's lines below. Guide him to understand that the Prince speaks mostly in commands. We can infer that the Prince is used to having things done for him, telling others what to do, and having his orders carried out immediately. From his words, we may conclude that he is also fair and courteous.

- Guards! How dare you treat a poor lad like that! Release him!
- Well, that is better! Tell me more about your life at Offal Court. What do you do for fun there?
- Would you really like that? Then it shall be. I'll call the servants to clear the table. While they do that, you and I will have time to go into the next room and exchange clothing. *(Calls)* Page!

After the discussion, have your student predict what will happen to Prince Edward when he arrives at Tom Canty's house. Encourage him to support his prediction with evidence from the text. Point out to your student that the Prince's behavior will conflict with what the Cantys expect. You might ask:

Do you think the Prince will be willing to change his behavior when he gets to the Cantys' house? Why or why not? Should he?

Then have him write a paragraph in his Reading Notebook on the following topic:

Predict what will happen to Prince Edward while he is at the Canty house. (For example, how will the Prince react when John and Gammer Canty give him orders?) Explain your reasons for your prediction.

Lesson 3: "The Prince and the Pauper": Session 2

Tom and Prince Edward return, much wiser, to their familiar lives. Compare and contrast the main characters and read aloud or act out part of the play.

Lesson Notes
This is the second of two sessions on "The Prince and the Pauper" (A Play).

Objectives
Demonstrate comprehension of text.
Describe a character using evidence from the text.
Compare and contrast characters.
Identify the theme.

Student Pages
"The Prince and the Pauper" (A Play): Session 2
Compare and Contrast Characters

Materials
crayons, markers, or colored pencils

1. Get Ready

Vocabulary
Go over the vocabulary words with your student before he reads the story.

> **cackle:** (v.) to laugh harshly or cruelly
> "Too bad you can't come to the ball," Cinderella's wicked stepsisters *cackled*, slamming the door as they left.

> **fatigue:** (n.) exhaustion
> After running twenty miles to deliver the letter, the messenger collapsed with *fatigue*.

> **reluctantly:** (adv.) not willingly
> Bobby made a very sour face as he *reluctantly* ate his spinach.

> **impostor:** (n.) a person pretending to be someone else
> The wolf tried to sneak into the flock by wearing a sheep skin, but when the sheep saw his hairy paws, they knew he was an *impostor*.

> **imperiously:** (adv.) commandingly
> He spoke so *imperiously* that everyone rushed to follow his orders.

> **ward:** (n.) a person who is guarded or protected
> "You shall be my *wards*," said the knight to the orphans, "and I promise you shall always have food to eat, clothes to wear, and a safe place to live.".

> **bearing:** (n.) the way a person acts or carries himself
> He had such a noble *bearing* that everyone who saw him was filled with admiration.

Think Ahead

1. Summarize the first two scenes of "The Prince and the Pauper."

   Tip: To prepare your student for the assessment at the end of the unit, make sure he includes the following information in his summary:
   - How Tom and the Prince meet (they meet when Tom goes to try to see the Prince)
   - What they decide to do (they decide to exchange clothes)
   - What is unusual about the boys' appearances (they look alike)
   - How they get separated (the Prince goes out to speak to the guards, they mistake him for Tom, and Tom's father brings the Prince back to Offal Court)

2. Describe Tom and the Prince. How are they alike and different?
   Words to describe Tom might include: humble, polite, kind, and truthful. Words to describe Prince Edward might include: commanding, just, friendly, and sympathetic.

   Tip: Remind your student that Tom and Prince Edward look alike, but discuss the differences in their upbringing and behavior. For example, the Prince is used to giving orders and having others tend to him, while Tom is used to unkindness from his father and grandmother, and mostly takes care of himself.

2. Read

Have your student read Scenes 3 and 4 of "The Prince and the Pauper" in *Classics for Young Readers*, Vol. 5A, pages 101-108.

3. Questions

Have your student write the answers to the questions in his Reading Notebook. If he has difficulty, have him read the relevant part of the story aloud.

1. How do the Cantys treat the Prince?
   Tom's father and grandmother beat the Prince. But Tom's mother tries to stop them, tries to help him, and makes him soup.

2. What do Hugo and Ruffler tell the Prince that surprises him?
   Hugo and Ruffler tell the Prince that many innocent people are in prison, and some are punished even when they have not committed a crime.

3. What question does Lord St. John ask the Prince that proves he is telling the truth?
   Lord St. John asks the Prince where the Great Seal is.

4. What happens to Tom at the end of the play?
   At the end of the play, Tom is made the King's Ward.

4. Discuss

Discuss today's reading. If you wish, have your student write a paragraph in response to one of the questions.

1. After changing places with Tom, what do you think the Prince learns? What do you think he will do differently in the future?
2. What do you think Tom learns after changing places with the Prince?

Tip: You may wish to point out that each boy thought the other had a better life and took some of the pleasures of his own life for granted. You might recall the saying, "The grass is always greener on the other side." Discuss with your student what he thinks the phrase means and how it might apply to Tom and Prince Edward.

5. Activities

Compare and Contrast Characters

Have your student compare and contrast Tom Canty and Prince Edward. First have him complete the chart on page 1 of the Compare and Contrast Characters page. If necessary, help him find the following information in the texts (both the selections from the novel and the play):

- What each boy's life is like before they trade places (For example: Before Tom trades places with the Prince, he dreams of royalty but has to beg for food. Before trading places with Tom, the Prince knows nothing of poverty. He only knows kindness.)

- A description of each boy's character, with examples from the text to support his opinion (For example: Tom is honest. When the Prince comes back to claim the throne, even though the Prince's life was nicer than Tom's, Tom tells the truth. The Prince is caring. He is bothered that Tom's grandmother beats him.)

- Something each boy learns by trading places (For example: The Prince learns that there is injustice and unhappiness in his kingdom, and he promises, as King, to give justice to the people. Tom learns more about the responsibilities and conduct of a king.)

When he finishes, discuss and have him write answers to the questions below on the blank lines. If your student has difficulty, brainstorm a list of ways the characters are alike or different, and then have your student choose the most important one from the list.

- Tom and Prince Edward look alike. But, in your opinion, what is the most important thing they have in common? (For example, each boy thinks the other has a better life, or both boys believe in the importance of fairness.)

- Tom is a pauper and Edward is a prince. But, in your opinion, what is the most important way they are different? (For example, Tom is willing to learn and follow the etiquette of the court, while Prince Edward will not eat the Cantys' soup without "proper service.")

Your student may draw a picture of each character when he finishes.

Optional: The Curtain Rises

Have your student read aloud or act out a portion of the play. Discuss with him which parts were most exciting, most unusual, or most important. Then have him choose the part of the play and the characters he would like to read. You can read the parts of other characters.

Next, have your student look back over his work, describe each character, and explain how each character is different from the others.

Have him rehearse his lines. He does not need to memorize the lines, though he may if he wishes. Remind him to pay attention to the stage directions.

For some students, speaking expressively is a challenge. Your student will enjoy and be inspired by hearing you model good, dramatic expressive speaking. Suggested discussion questions:

- How does this character feel during this part of the play? How can you say your line to show how the character feels?
- What do you think this character's voice sounds like?
- How does this character move?

Encourage him to read loudly and clearly. Sit at a distance from your student, as though you were in the audience. Is he speaking loudly and clearly enough for you to understand him? Encourage him to project so he can be heard and understood.

Lesson 4: Unit Assessment

Check your student's recall and understanding with the unit assessment.

Lesson Notes

Make sure your student understands the directions for the Unit Assessment, then have him complete the assessment on his own. (He should not refer to the *Classics for Young Readers* book while doing the assessment.)

Objectives

Demonstrate comprehension of text.

Describe a character using evidence from the text.

Demonstrate cultural literacy by identifying authors, characters, and quotations from a variety of literary works.

Part 1: Facts About the Story

Answers:

1. b
2. b
3. a
4. d
5. c

Part 2: Describe a Character

Your student should write four paragraphs that identify and describe either Tom Canty or Edward Tudor and tell one thing the character learns from trading places. He should support each adjective he chooses with an example from the text.

Look back to your student's Reading Notebook entries and to his Compare and Contrast Characters page for examples of the descriptions and evidence he should write about.

Unit 4: Seasonal Change

The four seasons—each with its distinct sights, sounds, and smells, and each evoking a diverse range of feelings and memories—inspire poets in various ways. Your student will compare and contrast poems inspired by each of the seasons. She will recognize how the poets treat the same subject in different ways through varying uses of figurative and literal language.

Lesson 1: Summer

Your student will compare and contrast four poems about summer.

Objectives
Compare and contrast poems.
Distinguish figurative from literal language.
Recognize imagery in poems.

Student Pages
Summer
Describing Summer

Materials
Classics for Young Readers, Vol. 5A, "June" (page 128), "That Was Summer" (page 131), "Summer Rain" (page 129), and "Summer Rain" (page 130)

Keywords
imagery: language that appeals to the senses, that makes readers see, hear, smell, taste, or feel things in their imagination, for example: "the coal-black night," "the stinging cold," "the rapping and tapping of rain on the roof"

literal language: words used plainly and factually, for their exact, standard meaning

figurative language: language that uses figures of speech, such as metaphor, simile, and personification, for poetic effect rather than for precise, factual meaning. For example: "Her eyes are stars" is figurative language, in contrast to the literal use of "stars" in "The stars are shining tonight."

simile (SIH-muh-lee): a figure of speech that compares two things, usually using the words *like* or *as,* for example: "like a thief in the night," "quiet as a mouse"

metaphor: a figure of speech that suggests or states a comparison between two unlike things, without using such words as *like* or *as*, for example: "The cat's eyes were emeralds shining in the night"; or, "The wind was a torrent of darkness among the gusty trees, / The moon was a ghostly galleon tossed upon cloudy seas." (from "The Highwayman" by Alfred Noyes)

First Reading: "June" and "That Was Summer"

1. Get Ready

Think Ahead

Ask your student to explain what it means to compare or contrast something. (To compare is to examine in order to notice similarities and differences; to contrast is to show differences.) Give her an example of two things to compare. You might choose two pets in your household or two members of the family. Have your student describe the differences and similarities she sees.

Talk with your student about summer. When she thinks about this season, what colors, images, or scenes come to mind?

2. Read

Have your student read "June" and "That Was Summer" once silently and a second time aloud. (You may want to read the poems aloud first.)

3. Questions

1. In your own words, describe what is happening in each poem.
    In "June," it is a warm, breezy summer day and the speaker is taking off his shoes to go barefoot through the grass. In "That Was Summer," the poet is remembering smells associated with summer.

2. Write the names of each of your five senses.
    sight, hearing, touch, smell, taste

3. Both poems appeal to your senses. But each poem appeals to a different sense. "That Was Summer" is mostly about smells. What summery smells does the poet describe?
    The summery smells include: the smell of the warm soil and the grass, a steamy sidewalk after a sudden storm, the bark of a tree, and the smell of "sunshine" from a shirt worn while playing outside all day.

4. Have you ever done what the speaker in "June" is doing? What does it feel like to walk barefoot in grass?
    Answers will vary.

5. Which of your senses does "June" mostly appeal to? Point to words and lines in the poem that appeal to this sense.
    "June" appeals to the sense of touch (the feeling of the "warm" breeze, the feeling of going barefoot) and the sense of sight (the "blue" sky, the "glowing eye" that is the sun, the "green" of growing things).

6. These two poems are alike because they appeal to your senses. They are different because each poem appeals to a different sense. In what other ways are these poems different?

Answers will vary. They could include: one poem is shorter than the other; one poem has rhyming words, the other doesn't; one poem is about memory while the other describes a present moment.

Second Reading: Two Poems Called "Summer Rain"

4. Get Ready

Vocabulary

Go over the vocabulary words with your student before she reads the next pair of poems

scythe: (n.) a tool for cutting grain
The farmer used a *scythe* to cut the wheat.

uproar: (n.) loud, noisy excitement
There was an *uproar* in the gym after the home team won the game.

pageant: (n.) a parade, or a fancy play or celebration
In the Christmas *pageant,* I played the part of a shepherd.

dread: (adj.) causing great fear
The young knight trembled as he approached the cave of the *dread* dragon.

tread: (n.) heavy step
Jack could hear the Giant's *tread* behind him as he started to climb down the beanstalk.

tangy: (adj.) having a sharp, pleasant flavor
I enjoyed the *tangy* taste of the lemonade.

Think Ahead

Discuss the difference between *literal* and *figurative* language. When you speak literally, you use words for their plain, everyday, factual meanings. But when you speak figuratively, as poets often do, you use words in unusual and imaginative ways. Point out that we often use figurative language even in everyday speech. For example:

Literal: My pillow is soft.
Figurative: My pillow feels like a big, puffy cloud.

Literal: Coach Anderson yells a lot but he's really a nice man.
Figurative: Coach Anderson yells a lot, but he's really just a big teddy bear.

Literal: You broke Mom's favorite lamp. Now you're really in trouble!
Figurative: You broke Mom's favorite lamp. Now you're really in hot water!

Tip: The general category of figurative language includes a variety of figures of speech and poetic devices, including simile, metaphor, personification, onomatopoeia, and more. If your student has studied literature in the earlier grades of K12's Language Arts curriculum, she has already encountered these terms, and will encounter them again through the fifth grade lessons on poetry. Depending on your student's familiarity with these terms, you may only need to briefly review them, or you may wish to pause and discuss them in more detail.

5. Read

Have your student read both poems titled "Summer Rain" once silently and a second time aloud. (You may want to read the poems aloud first.) Start with the poem by Elizabeth Coatsworth.

6. Questions

1. In the first poem, where do you think the people are standing?
    In Elizabeth Coatsworth's "Summer Rain," the people are probably standing in a house, looking through a window ("through the pane") at the rainstorm outside.

2. Which of your five senses does the first stanza of the first poem most appeal to? Point to specific words or phrases that appeal to this sense.
    The first stanza appeals most to the sense of hearing, with words such as "sweet uproar" and "tapping and rapping."

3. Which words in the second poem appeal to your five senses?
    Answers will vary. For example: Hearing: "tinkle"; Sight: "greensilver," "a million-dot freckle," "spotted"; Taste: "tangy"; Smell: "cinnamon"; Touch: "tingles," "tickle."

4. The second poem describes the rain as "a shower, a sprinkle." Is that *literal* or *figurative* language?
    literal

5. The second poem also says that the rain is "like stars on your toes" and like "a million-dot freckle." Is that *literal* or *figurative* language?
    figurative

Activities

7. Figurative Language: Imagery, Metaphor, and Simile

Tell your student that the poems she read today use *imagery*. Imagery is language that appeals to the senses, that makes readers see, hear, smell, taste, or feel things in their imagination, for example:

*   the rain "tapping and rapping wildly at the door" (from "Summer Rain" by Elizabeth Coatsworth)
*   "Remember how the pavement smelled – all steamy warm and wet?" (from "That Was Summer")

Imagery can include two specific kinds of figurative language: simile and metaphor. If these terms are new to your student, first discuss the definitions and examples below.

*   simile (SIH-muh-lee): a figure of speech that compares two things, usually using the words *like* or *as,* for example: "like a thief in the night," "quiet as a mouse"

- metaphor: a figure of speech that suggests or states a comparison between two unlike things, without using such words as *like* or *as*, for example: "The cat's eyes were emeralds shining in the night"; or "The wind was a torrent of darkness among the gusty trees, / The moon was a ghostly galleon tossed upon cloudy seas." (from "The Highwayman" by Alfred Noyes)

Have your student look for examples of metaphor and simile in the two poems titled "Summer Rain." Discuss how the similes and metaphors work and how they help us see and imagine the rain.

In "Summer Rain" by Elizabeth Coatsworth:
Simile:

> cutting across the heat as scythes cut across grain
> the lightning, like a tiger

Metaphor:

> the circus pageant of the rain
> the thunder cross the shaken sky with elephant tread

In "Summer Rain" by Eve Merriam:
Simile:

> Like salt on your nose,
> Like stars on your toes…

> Like a cinnamon
> Geranium

Metaphor:

> A tangle
> A tickle
> A million-dot freckle

8. Describing Summer

Have your student complete the Describing Summer page. Emphasize that she can describe the whole season, or just some specific aspect of it, such as a special place (for example, the beach) or a favorite event (such as the 4th of July, with picnics, parades, and fireworks). Encourage her to use figurative language that appeals to the senses. Her description, whether a poem or a paragraph, should have at least one simile or metaphor. When she finishes, encourage her to read her description aloud.

Lesson 2: Autumn

Your student will compare and contrast four poems about autumn.

Objectives
Compare and contrast poems.
Distinguish figurative from literal language.
Recognize imagery, simile, and personification in poems.

Student Pages
Autumn
Painting a Picture of Fall

Materials
Classics for Young Readers, Vol. 5A, "The City of Falling Leaves" (page 133), "The Leaves Do Not Mind at All" (page 134), "Autumn Woods" (page 135), and "Fall" (page 136)

Optional: crayons, colored pencils, chalk, or watercolors

Keyword
personification: giving human qualities to a thing or abstraction, for example: "The kettle sang on the hearth"; or "After the victory, freedom held its head high in the nation."

First Reading: "The City of Falling Leaves" and "The Leaves Do Not Mind at All"

1. Get Ready

Think Ahead
Talk with your student about autumn. When she thinks about this season, what colors, images, or scenes come to mind?

Remind your student what it means to *compare* and *contrast.* Also review the difference between *literal* and *figurative* language. The given examples— "the wind sang through the branches," "the leaves danced in the breeze"—are figurative language. You might contrast these with literal statements, such as, "The wind blew" or "the leaves fell."

Tip: "The City of Falling Leaves" refers to the city of Venice, a port city in northeast Italy. While it's not necessary to know anything about Venice in order to appreciate the poem, you might want to have your child locate Venice on a map or globe.

2. Read

Have your student read "The City of Falling Leaves" and "The Leaves Do Not Mind at All" once silently and a second time aloud. (You may want to read the poems aloud first.)

3. Questions

1. In your own words, describe what is happening in each poem.
    "The City of Falling Leaves": Leaves are falling in the city of Venice.
    "The Leaves Do Not Mind at All": Leaves are flying through the air and falling to the ground where they settle under a rail.

2. What are the colors of the leaves in "The City of Falling Leaves"? Which verbs show how the leaves fall? Is this description of the falling leaves mostly *literal* or *figurative*?
    Colors: "brown streaked with yellow"; "yellow streaked with brown." Verbs that show how the leaves fall: *fall, flutter,* and *drift.* The description is mostly literal.

3. In "The Leaves Do Not Mind at All," the leaves almost seem to be human. For example, they "don't mind" that they are falling. Can you find other lines in the poem that describe something the leaves do that a person would usually do?
    The leaves "put on a traveling coat." They "used to hear" a "noisy little pool" that they now can "see." They get "tired out" and "creep / Under some friendly rail and go to sleep."

4. In "The Leaves Do Not Mind at All," are the descriptions of the falling leaves mostly *literal* or *figurative*?
    The descriptions are mostly figurative.

5. In "The Leaves Do Not Mind at All," the poet uses a *simile* to describe a falling leaf. A simile compares two things, usually using the words *like* or *as.* What is the simile in this poem?
    The simile in the poem compares a leaf to a bird: "swiftly on the wing, / Like a bird adventuring."

Second Reading: "Autumn Woods" and "Fall"

4. Get Ready

Vocabulary
Go over this vocabulary word with your student before she reads the poems.

withered: (adj.) dried up
My mother emptied the vase and threw away the *withered* flowers.

Think Ahead
Talk with your student again about autumn. Ask her how the beginning of a season like autumn can be very different from the end of that same season.

5. Read

Have your student read "Autumn Woods" and "Fall" once silently and a second time aloud. (You may want to read the poems aloud first.)

6. Questions

1. In "Autumn Woods," what does the speaker like best about autumn? What can he do in autumn that he cannot do at any other time of the year?

    > He likes it when the wind blows and all the leaves have fallen off the trees so he can make a "bed of dry leaves," perhaps to jump into or lie down in.

2. Which of your senses does "Autumn Woods" appeal to? Point to words and lines in the poem that appeal to these senses.

    > Hearing: "wind sweeps by with a lonesome rushing sound," "rustle." Touch: "thick dry leaves"

3. In "Fall," the people "lock the garden gate" and "put the swings away." They already have taken the screens off the windows and put them in the attic and taken all the toys and outdoor furniture off the porch. What are they preparing for?

    > They are preparing for snow and the coming of winter.

4. In "Fall," the poet uses the words "withered," "deserted," and "alone." What do you feel like when you hear words like this?

    > Answers will vary.

5. Is the language in these two poems more *literal* or *figurative*?

    > The language in these poems is more literal.

Activities

7. Personification

Personification is another kind of figurative language. Remind your student that language that gives human traits or characteristics to non-human things or ideas is called *personification*. If this term is new to your student, pause to discuss the definition and examples of personification below.

Write the word and ask your student to underline or highlight the *person* in *personification.* To *personify* is to make a thing seem like a person. When a writer gives human characteristics to things that are not human, we call this personification.

Discuss the following examples. Point out, for example, that wind can blow, but people knock; the sun can shine, but people smile.

Literal language	Personification (figurative language)
The wind blew hard.	The wind knocked at the door.
The sun is shining.	The sun is smiling down on us.

8. Painting a Picture of Fall

Have your student complete the Painting a Picture of Fall page. As needed, review the terms *imagery, simile, metaphor,* and *personification.* If your student wishes to do the optional part of the activity—drawing or painting a fall scene—she will need crayons, colored pencils, chalk, or watercolors.

Lesson 3: Winter

Your student will compare and contrast four poems about winter.

Objectives
Compare and contrast poems.
Recognize figurative and literal language.
Identify tone.

Student Pages
Winter
Winter at Your Fingertips

Materials
Classics for Young Readers, Vol. 5A, "Winter the Huntsman" (page 137), "Falling Snow" (page 138), "On a Snowy Day" (page 139), and "Snowflakes" (page 139)

Keywords
tone: the attitude or emotion conveyed in speaking or writing. For example, the tone is happy, lively, and excited in the opening lines of Karla Kuskin's "Spring": "I'm shouting / I'm singing / I'm swinging through the trees." Compare that with the sad, gloomy tone in the opening lines of Judith Viorst's "Since Hanna Moved Away": "The tires on my bike are flat. / The sky is grouchy gray. / At least it sure feels like that / Since Hanna moved away."

First Reading: "Winter the Huntsman" and "Falling Snow"

1. Get Ready

Vocabulary
Go over these vocabulary words with your student before she reads the poems.

asunder: (adj.) apart, into pieces
The lightning bolt struck the tree trunk and tore it *asunder*.

reynard: (n.) the name for a fox in some legends and fables
Mr. Tod is the *reynard* in Beatrix Potter tales.

glade: (n.) an open space in a forest
As we walked through the woods, we came upon a pleasant *glade,* and there we had our picnic.

Think Ahead
Talk with your student about winter. When she thinks about this season, what colors, images, or scenes come to mind?

Ask her if she can tell the difference between the *tone* of your voice when you are pleased about something and the tone of your voice when you are angry about something. Tell her poets and writers use *tone* to give clues about how they feel about the things they are describing. Tell her to be on the lookout for words that reveal *tone* in the poems she will read today. As needed, remind your student what the terms *figurative* and *literal,* and *compare* and *contrast* mean.

2. Read

Have your student read "Winter the Huntsman" and "Falling Snow" once silently and a second time aloud. (You may want to read the poems aloud first.)

3. Questions

1. In "Winter the Huntsman," winter is described as a Huntsman on horseback, crashing through the woods, tearing apart things in his path. This is a *figurative* description. In your own words, describe what *literally* is happening in the poem.

   The poem describes the fierce onset of winter: autumn colors fade, trees are left bare when leaves fall, winds tear branches from limbs, animals creep into their shelters, darkness descends.

2. How would you describe the tone of this poem? Is it harsh or pleasant? Point to specific verbs and sounds in the poem that create a pleasant or harsh tone.

   The tone is harsh: "hooves crash and thunder"; "bare trees shiver"; "dying sound"; "cruel whip"

3. Much of the imagery in "Winter the Huntsman" appeals to your sense of hearing. Point to words and lines in the poem that appeal to this sense.

   "sighing"; "crash and thunder"; "cracking"

4. In your own words, describe what is happening in "Falling Snow." Is the poet describing the falling snow literally or figuratively?

   The poem describes snow falling on and around a house. The descriptions are literal. The snow falls thickly and softly onto the house, the garden, the trees, and the grass, transforming things to white that were green, brown, and black.

5. Does the poet in "Falling Snow" like the snow? Which words are your clues?

   The poet likes the snow. The falling snowflakes are "pretty," "soft," and "white." The poet says "What a pretty sight!"

6. Compare the *tone* of the two poems. Which poem has a more negative tone about winter? Which poem has a more positive tone?

   "Winter the Huntsman" has a more negative tone—harsh, violent, dark. "Falling Snow" has a more positive tone—happy, calm, delighted.

Second Reading: "On a Snowy Day" and "Snowflakes"

4. Get Ready

Think Ahead

Talk with your student about snow. If your student has seen snow falling, ask her if falling snow always looks the same. Have her describe different kinds of snowfalls from flurries to blizzards. Then ask your student to close her eyes and imagine a sandbox full of toys—bulldozers, shovels, pails—all covered with fluffy, white snow. What would these snow-covered objects look like? Encourage her to use her imagination!

5. Read

Have your student read "On a Snowy Day" and "Snowflakes" once silently and a second time aloud. (You may want to read the poems aloud first.)

6. Questions

1. You just imagined what toys covered with snow in a sandbox might look like. What are the *literal* snow-covered objects the poet describes in "Snowy Days"?

    The snow-covered objects are fence posts, bushes, and trees.

2. The snow changes the way these objects look, doesn't it? The poet *personifies* them in the poem—she describes them acting or doing things like people. Point to the words and lines that describe the snow-covered objects in these human ways.

    Fence posts *wearing* hats; bushes *kneeling* down; trees *spreading out* skirts and *dancing*.

3. In both poems, the poets use *metaphor* to describe the snow and snowflakes. They compare the snow to unlike things. Find at least one metaphor in each poem. Explain what each metaphor is comparing.

    In "On a Snowy Day," the poet compares the snow to "marshmallow hats," "nightgowns," and "snowy skirts." In "Snowflakes," the poet compares snowflakes to "feathers" from the chickens of "the Moon Lady," and to "a baby star."

4. How would you describe the tone of these two poems? Do the poets seem to like the subjects they are writing about?

    The tone of both poems might be described as happy, lively, playful, or gentle. The poets seem to like the snow.

Activities

7. Winter at Your Fingertips: An Extended Metaphor

Discuss with your student the basic metaphor captured in the title of "Winter the Huntsman" (Winter = Huntsman). Then help your student see how the poet extends this metaphor throughout the poem. The huntsman rides a horse whose hooves "crash and thunder" through the woods; the huntsman blows his "sighing" horn and "cracks his cruel whip." Nature reacts to this huntsman and horse by retreating into holes or hiding in shadows.

Have your student complete the Winter at Your Fingertips page to prepare for creating her own extended metaphor about winter.

Lesson 4: Spring

Your student will compare and contrast four poems about spring.

Objectives

Compare and contrast poems.
Recognize figurative and literal language.
Recognize simile, metaphor, personification, and imagery.
Identify tone.

Student Pages

Spring
Spring Has Sprung

Materials

Classics for Young Readers, Vol. 5A, "April" (page 140), "April" (page 140), "In the Time of Silver Rain" (page 141), and "Spring" (page 142)

First Reading: Two Poems Called "April"

1. Get Ready

Vocabulary

Go over this vocabulary word with your student before she reads the first pair of poems.

> **save:** (conjunction) an old-fashioned word for "but" or "except"
> I would love to visit Africa *save* that I am scared to fly.

Think Ahead

Talk with your student about spring. When she thinks about this season, what colors, images, or scenes come to mind? How is the beginning of spring different from the end of spring?

2. Read

Have your student read both poems titled "April" once silently and a second time aloud. (You may want to read the poems aloud first.)

3. Questions

1. Both poems are called "April" and describe the beginning of spring, but each poem describes a different scene. In your own words, describe these two scenes.
    In the first poem, it is rainy, windy, and birds are "twittering." There is no new spring growth, but the speaker senses that spring is in the air. In the second poem, there is also wind and a bird, but here a tulip and new grass are growing.

2. Which of your senses does the first "April" poem appeal to? Point to the words and lines in the poem that appeal to these senses.

Sight: "shining" and "bare and brown." Hearing: "twitter"

3. Which of your senses does the second "April" poem appeal to? Point to the words and lines in the poem that appeal to these senses.

   Sight: "tulips pushing up"; "robin taking a look around." Hearing: "spring laughing with a windy sound"

4. In the second poem the poet uses a *simile* to describe the tulips pushing up through the ground. What two things does she compare in this simile?

   She compares the tulips just beginning to grow to "small green knuckles" that are "pushing up...through the ground."

5. Explain the use of *personification* in the last line of the second poem.

   The poet gives the season human qualities by describing "Spring *laughing* with a windy sound."

Second Reading: "In Time of Silver Rain"

4. Get Ready

Think Ahead

Have your student describe a time she remembers walking in the rain. Talk with her about the "color" of the rain.

Tip: You might recall from an earlier lesson that in "Summer Rain," the poet Eve Merriam made up a word to describe the color of the rain: "Greensilver runs the rain."

5. Read

Have your student read "In Time of Silver Rain" once silently and a second time aloud. (You may want to read the poem aloud first.)

6. Questions

1. When you think of the word "silver," what images come to mind? The poet describes a spring rain as "silver." What do you think he means?

   Answers will vary. For example: Silver is bright and shiny. It implies riches and wealth. In the old saying, "Every cloud has a silver lining," silver is associated with good things happening.

2. In this poem, the flowers are blooming, the green grass is growing, butterflies are flying, and trees are putting forth new leaves. How is this description different from the spring described in the last two poems you read?

   The flowers and trees were not as far along in the other two poems. This poem describes spring later in the season, when winter is definitely over and life is bursting forth everywhere.

3. At the end of the first stanza, why do you think the poet repeats "Of life" three times?

   Answers will vary. For example: The poet wants to celebrate life. He is filled with wonder and happiness at the sight of everything coming back to life.

4. What sounds of spring does the poet describe in the second stanza? Which of these sounds are literal? (That is, which are real sounds?) Which are figurative? (That is, which are sounds you could only imagine?)

      Literal sounds: Boys and girls are singing. Figurative sounds: "a rainbow cry"; trees "sing in joy."

Third Reading: "Spring"

7. Get Ready

Vocabulary
Go over this vocabulary word with your student before she reads the next poem.

    gamboling: (v.) skipping about playfully
    We watched the playful ponies *gamboling* in the field.

Think Ahead
Review that a poet's attitude and emotions come through in the *tone* of a poem. Ask your student to think about the tone of the next poem.

8. Read

Have your student read "Spring" once silently and a second time aloud. (You may want to read the poem aloud first.)

9. Questions

1. Instead of describing spring itself, this poem describes a person's reaction to spring. In the poem, the speaker does many things to welcome spring. What are some of these actions? (Hint: look for vivid verbs.)
    shouting, singing, swinging, winging, gamboling

2. Which of these actions are things a person *literally* (really) could do?
    shouting, singing, kicking up heels, racing through meadows without any coat

3. Which of these actions are *figurative?* That is, which describe things a person could only imagine doing?
    winging skyhigh, running on rooftops

4. The speaker uses *metaphor* to describe how she feels. She compares herself to other things. For example, she says, "I'm a rabbit." Point to other metaphors in the poem.
    The speaker says she is "the sun," "the moon," "dew on a rose," "a gamboling lamb," "a light leaping goat," "a bud," "a bloom," and "a dove on the wind."

5. How would you describe the *tone* of the poem? Does the speaker like spring?
    The tone is joyous, playful, and exuberant. The speaker *loves* spring!

Activity

10. Spring Has Sprung: Differences in Tone

Have your student complete the Spring Has Sprung page.

Remind your student that, as the poem called "Spring" makes clear, verbs can greatly influence the tone of a poem. For example, a bird can *squawk* and *screech* or it can *twitter* and *serenade*. A child can *march, stomp,* or *skip.* Rain can *tickle* or *sting.* Encourage your student to choose his words carefully, and to pay special attention to verbs.

Lesson 5: Unit Assessment

Have your student complete the Unit 4 Assessment. After your student completes the assessment, enter the results online.

Objectives
Compare and contrast stanzas about similar subject matter.
Define simile and metaphor.
Recognize simile and metaphor.
Define personification.
Define tone.
Define literal and figurative language.
Distinguish between literal and figurative language.

Definitions and Identifications

Answers:
1. c
2. e
3. b
4. d
5. f
6. a
7. figurative
8. literal
9. underline "the circus pageant of the rain" circle: "like a tiger"

Compare and Contrast

Answers will vary but should include a number of these points:
- Both describe winter.
- Each has a different tone.
- Winter is cruel and harsh in the first stanza.
- The snow is pretty and pleasant in the second stanza.
- The first stanza uses metaphor to describe the winter.
- The second stanza describes the falling snow more literally.

Unit 5: Curious Creatures

What sets nonfiction apart from other types of writing? Explore the characteristics of the nonfiction genre. Get to know the parts of a nonfiction book, such as the table of contents, glossary, and index. Learn to distinguish between fact and opinion.

Lesson 1: "Eating Like a Bird": Session 1

Learn about the unusual ways birds at the Merritt Island National Wildlife Refuge catch their meals. Identify the unstated main idea of an article and categorize details.

Lesson Notes

This is the first of two sessions on "Eating Like a Bird." Please save all of your students projects from this unit because he will need to refer to them when he reaches the semester review and assessment.

Objectives

Demonstrate comprehension of the text.
Identify characteristics of nonfiction.
Locate and use the table of contents.
Identify the main idea.
Classify and categorize details.

Student Pages

"Eating Like a Bird": Session 1
Details Chart

Materials

"Eating Like a Bird," *Curious Creatures*, pages 3-7
1 index card

1. Get Ready

Vocabulary

Ask your student what is missing from the first of today's vocabulary words. Tell him that the definition is missing because this book has a *glossary*. A glossary is a list of unfamiliar words in the book and their definitions.

Have your student use the table of contents to locate the glossary in the book. Explain that a glossary is almost always in the back of a book. Then go over the vocabulary words using the definitions from the glossary.

> **marsh:** (n.)
> When our ball rolled into the *marsh*, we knew not to go after it because we couldn't tell how deeply we would sink into the soggy ground.

> **crustacean:** (n.) a small water animal with a hard shell
> Crabs, shrimp, and lobsters are three kinds of *crustaceans*.

mammal: (n.) a warm-blooded animal that has hair and whose young are fed with milk
Many people think that whales are fish, but they are warm-blooded, have hair, and feed their young with milk, so they are *mammals*.

prey: (n.) the hunted animal
The lioness silently followed the herd of gazelles, waiting for the right moment to pounce on her *prey*.

roseate: (adj.) light reddish-pink
The flamingo is a *roseate* bird, almost the color of cotton candy.

Think Ahead
Discuss the following with your student.

1. What do you think you will learn about as you read the magazine? Do you think the articles are *fiction* or *nonfiction*? Why?

    As needed, remind your student that fictional stories are made up and nonfiction is based on fact. You might ask your student to name two or three stories from *Classics for Young Readers*. Explain that the *Classics* stories have one thing in common: they are all *fiction*. Fiction refers to stories that are created in the imagination or made up.

    Have your student look through the magazine. Ask him how it is different from the books and stories he has read so far. Have him point out any unusual features he notices. Guide him to notice features such as the table of contents, glossary, and index.

    Tell your student that *Curious Creatures* is a collection of five articles about animals. An article is a short piece of writing about a subject. Explain that even though each article is about a different subject, all of the articles have something in common: they are all about animals and they are factual. If a piece of writing is based on facts, or gives facts and information, it is called *nonfiction*.

    Introduce the following characteristics of nonfiction:
    1. It tells about a subject that really exists.
    2. It provides factual details about the subject.
    3. It often includes visuals such as graphs, maps, tables, timelines, diagrams, or photographs.

    Brainstorm with your student different kinds of nonfiction writing, for example, newspaper, magazine, or encyclopedia articles, travel guides, recipes, and letters.

2. Are there any special parts to the magazine? Is the magazine divided into chapters?

    Explain to your student that many forms of nonfiction writing have features that help a reader find information quickly. *Curious Creatures* has a table of contents, a glossary, and an index.

    As necessary, explain that the table of contents will allow him to easily locate which page each article begins on. The glossary is a dictionary containing meanings of some key words found in the book. Have him locate the glossary. The index is the last part of the book and contains key words and concepts with page numbers next to each. For example, if he wants to learn more about crustaceans, he can use the index to find out which pages mention the topic.

3. Have your student look up "Eating Like a Bird" in the table of contents to find the page numbers of the article.

2. Read

Have your student read "Eating Like a Bird," *Curious Creatures,* pages 3-7.

3. Questions

Have your student write the answers to the questions in his Reading Notebook. If he has difficulty, have him read the relevant part of the story aloud.

1. Explain what the expression "eating like a bird" means. Is this true of the birds in the selection?
    Eating like a bird means being a light, picky eater. The birds described in the selection are hungry and they work hard for their meals.

2. Describe three ways birds in the article catch their food.
    Some birds are waders. They stand in shallow water and grab little animals out of the water with their beaks. Some birds follow their food. They will dive underwater. Other birds drop down onto their prey. They fly down and scoop up the fish.

4. Discuss

Discuss today's reading. If you wish, have your student write a paragraph in response to one of the questions.

1. What do all the birds in the article have in common?
2. Which bird do you think is the most interesting? Why?

Tip: If your student has difficulty with the first question, have him read aloud the third paragraph of the article, which begins, "What all these birds have in common is a good appetite."

5. Activities

What's the Main Idea?
As needed, remind your student that the *main idea* in a piece of writing is the most important point the author makes. Finding the main idea can help a reader remember important information about the topic.

Point out that in many articles, the main idea is stated in a sentence in the first paragraph. However, in some articles, the main idea is unstated. Tell your student that *unstated* means "not said." When a main idea is unstated, it is not written in any one sentence.

Tell your student that he can discover the unstated main idea by reading all the sentences in the paragraph and deciding what they have in common. Help him find the unstated main idea in the following example:

Blind men and women use guide dogs to help them navigate busy city streets. Therapy dogs visit hospitals to bring cheer to patients. Hundreds of people lost in mountains or forests have been saved by rescue dogs.

Responses may vary, but should focus on the fact that dogs do important jobs that help people. If your student has difficulty finding the unstated main idea, guide him to recognize that:

- All the sentences are about dogs.
- All the sentences are about jobs dogs can do.
- All of the jobs mentioned have to do with helping people.

Have your student reread the first paragraph of "Eating Like a Bird" to find the unstated main idea. Have him tell three facts about birds from the paragraph, such as: "Some birds along the Florida seashore dive into the sea to catch their food," or "Birds along the Florida seashore do not 'eat like birds,' they don't just pick at their food." Discuss with him what the facts have in common. As necessary, guide him to recognize that:

- "Eating like a bird" means not eating very much or picking at food.
- Birds that live along the Florida seashore do not eat that way.
- The birds must wade into marshes, chase fish underwater, or do 30-foot high dives into the sea for food.

Next, have him decide which of the following is the unstated main idea of the article:

1. There are many kinds of birds along the Florida seashore. (Tip: If your student chooses this answer, tell him that the paragraph does mention many kinds of birds. Direct his attention to the last sentence in the paragraph and ask him, "What does the paragraph say about the way these birds eat?")
2. Birds along the Florida seashore work hard for their food. (correct)
3. Birds can't fly when their feathers are soaked with water.

Have your student write the unstated main idea on the first lines of the Details Chart.

Details Chart

In this activity, your student will differentiate between the main idea and details and write details from the article on a chart.

Have your student write the unstated main idea of the article on the Details Chart page. Tell him that the author of the article explains three specific ways that birds along the Florida coastline catch their food. Have him name and describe each way. As necessary, he may refer to Question 2 in his Reading Notebook.

Explain that the three ways birds catch their food are *details*. Details give more information about the main idea. The main idea of the article states that birds along the Florida coastline work hard for their food. The author gives more information, or details, about how the birds work for their food. He says they wade, follow, or drop down on their prey.

Explain that the author also gives details about each way birds catch their food. He gives the names of the birds that fall into a particular category, tells about problems certain categories of birds must face, and gives more specific information about how each bird catches its prey. For example, "The ibis uses its long, curved beak to feel in the water and in the mud for tasty bites like small fish and crustaceans." Help your student find one detail about waders and write it in the appropriate column on the Details Chart. Then have your student complete the Details Chart. Save it for the next lesson.

Point out that he may use the photo captions to find details. As necessary, tell him that *captions* are words, phrases, or sentences that tell more information about the photograph, graph, or other visual. Captions are usually written under or beside the picture. When you read nonfiction, it is important to look for any and all information the author gives you for clues.

Lesson 2: "Eating Like a Bird": Session 2

Discuss the venues authors have to share nonfiction information. Reorganize the facts in the article to create a brochure for visitors to the Merritt Island National Wildlife Refuge.

Lesson Notes
This is the second of two sessions on "Eating Like a Bird."

Objectives
Demonstrate comprehension of the text.
Identify characteristics of nonfiction.
Identify the main idea and details.
Classify and categorize details.

Student Pages
"Eating Like a Bird": Session 2
Details Chart

Materials
"Eating Like a Bird," *Curious Creatures*, pages 3-7
1 piece of plain white paper
crayons, markers, or colored pencils
map of the United States

1. Get Ready

Think Ahead
Discuss the following with your student.

1. What is the difference between fiction and nonfiction?
   As necessary, remind your student that fiction is stories that are made up or created in the imagination; nonfiction is writing based upon facts.

2. What differences did you notice between the "Eating Like a Bird" article and some of the *Classics* stories you've read?
   Accept any reasonable response. For example: The *Classics* stories included make-believe characters and places, some of the *Classics* stories taught a lesson or had a moral, or the article included facts and information.

3. Summarize the article.
   This summary should include the main idea of the article: Birds along the Florida seashore work hard for their food. Your student may also include the three ways these birds catch their food: wading, dropping down on their prey, and following their prey.

4. Review your Details Chart. Which birds did you find most interesting? Why?

2. Discuss

Author's Purpose

Explain to your student that authors have many ways to present nonfiction information. You may wish to brainstorm a list, for example: books, newspaper, encyclopedia, or magazine articles, signs or posters, brochures, websites or computer programs, or fact cards. Point out that each presentation serves a specific audience, or group of readers. Consider why some methods may be more appropriate for a particular need than others. For example, you wouldn't use an encyclopedia article to tell the public that there is a new animal at the zoo.

Discuss with your student the following questions about the "Eating Like a Bird" article:

1. What did you like best about the article?
    Accept any reasonable response.

2. What did you notice about the way the article is organized?
    Accept any reasonable response. Point out that there is an introduction, a main idea, supporting details, and a conclusion.

3. Now pretend you are a visitor to the Merritt Island National Wildlife Refuge in Florida, taking a tour through the park. What changes would you make to the article to make it easier for a tourist to use? Why?
    Accept any reasonable response. Guide your student to understand that it would be hard for a tourist to find information quickly in the article. Help you student to think about ways in which the birds might be grouped together. What characteristics do they share? Have him use his Details Chart to see the shared characteristics of the birds.

3. Activity

Bird Watch Brochure

Have your student reorganize the information in "Eating Like a Bird" to make a brochure for tourists to the island. Point out that one way to present nonfiction information is to make a brochure that highlights the most important features of a place or thing. Review his Details Chart with him before beginning.

Your student will need to fold a piece of paper in thirds. If he has trouble, help him to prepare the brochure. Lay a piece of paper horizontally. Fold the right-hand third toward the middle and crease it. Then fold the left-hand third toward the middle so that it covers the right third. Make a crease. You should have a rectangular shaped brochure. When you open the left and right flaps, you should be looking at the whole sheet of paper, divided into thirds. As your student makes the brochure, you may wish to help him draw boxes or circles in which to draw pictures of birds or the map.

As your student follows the directions below, guide him to use the index at the back of the magazine to help him quickly find information in the article. As necessary, explain that the index is the last part of the book and contains key words and concepts with page numbers next to each. For instance, if he wants to learn more about the flip-and-catch method that some birds use to catch their food, he can use the index to find out which pages mention it. You may wish to guide him through this exercise.

Directions:

1. Fold a piece of paper in thirds. This will be your brochure.
2. Make a cover for the brochure.
3. Label each of the three inside pages "Birds That Wade," "Birds That Follow Their Prey," and "Birds That Drop Down on Their Prey."
4. On each of the three inside pages, write two or more sentences that describe how each category of bird catches its food, list two or more kinds of birds that find their food that way, and draw and label a picture of one of those birds.
5. On the page that folds over from the right, draw a map of Florida. Mark Merritt Island with a star. Underneath the map, write two or more sentences that persuade people to visit the wildlife refuge.

Optional: You may wish to direct your student to the official Merritt National Wildlife Refuge website, http://merrittisland.fws.gov/. Your student may do additional research for his brochure or enjoy looking at the pictures.

Lesson 3: "The Ocean's Cleaning Stations": Session 1

Read about the symbiotic relationship between host and cleaner fish in the ocean. Identify the unstated main idea, discuss the author's purpose, and rewrite the opening of an article.

Lesson Notes

This is the first of two sessions on "The Ocean's Cleaning Stations." This article focuses on the concept of symbiosis. In strictly scientific terms, symbiosis refers to a relationship between two organisms from which at least one of the organisms benefit. For this article, however, the term symbiosis refers to a relationship between two organisms from which both animals benefit.

Objectives

Demonstrate comprehension of the text.
Compare and contrast elements of nonfiction.
Locate and use the table of contents and glossary.
Identify the main idea.
Identify evidence that supports the main idea in the text.
Identify author's style.

Student Page

"The Ocean's Cleaning Stations": Session 1

Materials

Curious Creatures, pages 8-11 and 3-7

1. Get Ready

Vocabulary

Have your student use the glossary to look up the definitions to today's vocabulary words.

parasite: (n.)
The veterinarian gave my dog medicine so he would not get *parasites*.

fungus: (n.)
Two kinds of *fungus*, mushrooms and mold, grew in the dead tree stump.

gullet: (n.)
The bird took such a big bite that the food got stuck in his *gullet*.

Think Ahead

Discuss the following with your student.

1. Look up "The Ocean's Cleaning Stations" in the table of contents.
2. What other kinds of "cleaning stations" do you know about? What happens there? What do you think happens at an ocean cleaning station?

Tip: Point out to your student that reviewing facts you already know about a topic before you read can help you understand the text more easily.

2. Read

Have your student read "The Ocean's Cleaning Stations," pages 8-11.

3. Questions

Have your student write the answers to the questions in his Reading Notebook. If he has difficulty, have him read the relevant part of the story aloud.

1. What is a host fish? What is a cleaner fish?
   Host fish are fish that host parasites. These parasites need to be cleaned off by cleaner fish.

2. Why do host fish, such as eels and parrotfish, go to the cleaning stations?
   Host fish go to cleaning stations so the cleaner fish can remove parasites from their skin.

3. What do the cleaner fish do with the parasites they clean off the host fish?
   The cleaner fish eat the parasites they clean off.

4. What happens when all the cleaners are removed from an area?
   When all the cleaners are removed from an area, many fish die, and those that are left are covered with sores and fungus.

5. What does the word *symbiosis* mean?
   Symbiosis is a relationship that is helpful to both parties. Each offers the other a necessary or helpful service. In the case of the host and cleaner fish, the host fish offer the food, and the cleaner fish offer the service of cleaning.

4. Discuss

Discuss today's reading. If you wish, have your student write a paragraph in response to one of the questions.

1. Why do you think bonnet-mouths and parrotfish hang in the water with their heads or tails straight up when they want a cleaning?
2. How do fish that can change color help the cleaners? Do you think this is useful? Why?
3. Why do you think that some host fish shudder when they sense danger? How does this help the cleaner fish?

5. Activities

Simply Symbiosis

Review with your student that some pieces of writing have an *unstated main idea.* Use the following questions and suggestions to help your student discover the unstated main idea: Symbiosis improves the lives of host fish and cleaner fish.

- Why is the relationship between the host and cleaner fish unusual? What would you expect to happen?

- What does the author say about symbiosis?
- Sometimes you can find information about the main idea of an article in the last paragraph. Read the last paragraph aloud. Describe the information the author gives. What is the author's main point?

Then have your student complete the Simply Symbiosis page. As necessary, help him find details in the text and remind him that to *draw a symbol* means to choose an object that stands for something else. For example, a symbol for the story "Cinderella" might be a glass slipper or a pumpkin coach.

Answers:
1. Accept any reasonable answer. For example: Symbiosis improves the lives of host and cleaner fish, or Symbiosis helps host and cleaner fish live longer and healthier.
2. In the relationship called symbiosis, each animal both gives and receives help from the other.
3. The cleaner fish removes parasites from the host fish.
4. The host fish's parasites make a meal for the cleaner fish.
5. No, the birds and fish do not have a symbiotic relationship.
6. The fish do not receive help from the birds. The birds eat the fish.
7. Accept any reasonable answer.

Author's Style
Point out that authors have many different choices in the way they begin their writing. Have your student reread the opening paragraph to both "The Ocean's Cleaning Stations" and "Eating Like a Bird." Use the following questions to help your student compare and contrast the paragraphs.

- Describe each beginning. Which beginning makes a connection between the reader and the subject matter?
- Which beginning sounds more like an eyewitness report?
- Which beginning includes questions?
- How does each beginning give hints to the unstated main idea?
- Which beginning is your favorite? Why?

Help your student see that the author of "The Ocean's Cleaning Stations" makes the beginning of her article sound like the actions are happening at just that moment. She draws readers in by making them wonder what will happen next between the eel and the goby fish.

Read the first sentence of "Eating Like a Bird" aloud. The author opens with a question to the reader. He asks, "Has anyone ever told you that you eat like a bird?" Do you think this is a good beginning? Both authors grab the reader's attention. The author of "Eating Like a Bird" draws readers in and hints at the main idea of the article – what does it mean to "eat like a bird"?

Have your student rewrite the beginning of "Eating Like a Bird" to make it sound like "The Ocean's Cleaning Stations." Have him choose his favorite bird from the article and find details about its method of catching food in the text. Then have him imagine or describe aloud what it would look like to see the bird catch its food.

Review with him the following example:

The brown pelican circles high in the sky, little more than a speck against the clouds. Suddenly, he drops out of the sky like a stone, plunges into the sea, and grabs a fish with his beak. This hungry predator certainly does not "eat like a bird." Nor do many of the other avian inhabitants of Merritt Island Wildlife Refuge, as you will see.

Point out that the author uses the phrase "eat like a bird" in her opening, and hints at the unstated main idea of the article: Some birds work very hard for their meals. Encourage your student to compare the bird to another thing, for example, a bird that uses flip-and-catch might be an "acrobat," or waders could stand "like statues."

Have your student write the opening in his Reading Notebook.

Lesson 4: "The Ocean's Cleaning Stations": Session 2

Discuss the venues authors have to share nonfiction information. Reorganize the facts in the article to create a travel guide for the ocean's cleaning stations for host and cleaner fish.

Lesson Notes

This is the second of two sessions on "The Ocean's Cleaning Stations."

Objectives

Demonstrate comprehension of the text.
Identify characteristics of nonfiction.
Classify and categorize details.
Locate information in a photo.

Student Page

"The Ocean's Cleaning Stations": Session 2

Materials

"The Ocean's Cleaning Stations," *Curious Creatures*, pages 8-11
3 pieces of plain white paper
crayons or colored pencils
stapler

1. Get Ready

Think Ahead

Discuss the following with your student.

1. What does *symbiosis* mean?
2. What does the host fish give and receive? The cleaner fish?
3. Why are cleaning stations so important?

2. Discuss

Author's Purpose

Explain to your student that authors have many ways to present nonfiction information. You may wish to brainstorm a list, for example: books, newspaper, encyclopedia, or magazine articles, signs or posters, brochures, websites or computer programs, or fact cards. Point out that each way serves a specific audience, or group of readers. Discuss with your student the following questions about "The Ocean's Cleaning Stations."

1. What did you like best about the article?
2. What did you notice about the way the article was organized?
3. If you wanted to give guidelines and directions for the ocean's cleaning stations, what changes would you make to this article? Why?

3. Activity

A Fish's Guide to the Ocean's Cleaning Stations

Have your student reorganize the information in "The Ocean's Cleaning Stations" to make a travel and how-to guide for host and cleaner fish. Point out that nonfiction information can be used to make instruction manuals of all kinds, from game or project directions to cookbooks to travel guides.

As your student follows the directions below, guide him to use the index at the back of the magazine to help him quickly find information in the article. As needed, explain that the index is the last part of the book and contains key words and concepts with page numbers next to each. For instance, if he wants to learn more about crustaceans, he can use the index to find out which pages mention it. You may wish to guide him through this exercise.

Point out that he may use the photo captions to help him find details. As needed, tell him that *captions* are words, phrases, or sentences that tell more information about the photograph, graph, or other visual. Captions are usually written under or beside the picture. He may also use the information in the photos to describe the cleaning process. When you read nonfiction, it is important to look for any and all information the author gives you for clues.

Directions:

1. Staple the three pieces of paper together to make a book.

2. Design the cover. Choose a title that tells what the guidebook is about, and write one or more sentences to persuade host and cleaner fish to go to the cleaning station.

3. On the first page, write a guide for host fish. Title the page, "For Host Fish," and write three or more sentences about each of the following:
   - When to Go: When and why should a host fish go for a cleaning?
   - How to Approach: How should the host fish swim as it approaches the cleaning station?
   - What Will Happen: What will happen when the host fish goes to the cleaning station?

4. On the back of the cover, draw a host fish. Use pictures from the article to help you.

5. On the second page, write a guide for cleaner fish. Title the page, "For Cleaner Fish," and write three or more sentences about each of the following:
   - Where to Go: How will a cleaner fish know which host fish are ready for a cleaning?
   - What Kind of Fish: What kinds of fish and shrimp are cleaners? What kinds of markings do cleaners have?
   - What to Do: What should a cleaner fish do when a host fish comes for cleaning? Is it safe? Why?

6. On the back of page 1, draw a cleaner fish. Use pictures from the article to help you.

7. On the back of the book, write a warning for false cleaners who might try to visit the cleaning station. You may illustrate this page if you wish.

Lesson 5: "Stormflight": Session 1

After a storm, termites in West Africa leave their mounds to establish new colonies. Identify the unstated main idea, and compare and contrast works of nonfiction.

Lesson Notes
This is the first of two sessions on "Stormflight."

Objectives
Demonstrate comprehension of the text.
Identify the main idea.
Locate and use the table of contents and glossary.
Compare and contrast characteristics of nonfiction.
Reorganize information into an outline.
Identify author's style.

Student Pages
"Stormflight": Session 1
It's All in the Details
Mighty Termites

Materials
Curious Creatures, pages 12-15

1. Get Ready

Vocabulary
Have your student use the glossary to look up the definitions to today's vocabulary words.

predator: (n.)
A hawk is a fierce *predator;* it dives down and catches rabbits, mice, and other rodents for its meals.

colony: (n.)
A *colony* of one hundred sparrows lives together in the same big tree.

bush: (n.) wild, undeveloped land
Animals in Africa do not live in cities or towns, they prefer to live in the *bush*.

Think Ahead
Discuss the following with your student.

1. Give two or more examples of kinds of nonfiction writing.
2. Look up "Stormflight" in the table of contents. Find the article and look at it. Do you notice anything different from the other articles you have read?

Tip: Guide your student to see the pull quote on page 13. He may also notice that the article contains illustrations rather than photographs, and there is a table of information on page 15. Explain that a pull quote is a very interesting statement that is pulled directly out of an article. It works like an advertisement for the article by telling the reader an interesting fact he will learn if he reads the piece. Pull quotes are written in a bigger font and offset with a box. Their purpose is to catch the reader's eye, engage him, and make him wonder about the statement so that he reads the article.

2. Read

Have your student read "Stormflight," pages 12-15.

3. Questions

Have your student write the answers to the questions in his Reading Notebook. If he has difficulty, have him read the relevant part of the story aloud.

1. In what month does the stormflight occur?
    The stormflight occurs in April.

2. What are the "plumes of steam"?
    The plumes of steam are flying termites.

3. Why are the conditions after the storm perfect for winged termites?
    It is wet after the storm, and termites need moisture. There is a breeze, so the termites can fly farther.

4. Explain what will happen to the termites that survive.
    The termites that survive will become kings and queens themselves and start their own colonies.

4. Discuss

Discuss today's reading. If you wish, have your student write a paragraph in response to one of the questions.

1. Reread the first paragraph of the article. Think about the last sentence: "You stand on the veranda of your mud-walled house, excited that the rains have finally come." The author of the article writes in a way that he puts you, the reader, in the middle of the action. Why do you think he writes the article in this way? Is it effective? Why or why not?

    Tip: Explain to your student that writing in this style is the author's way of drawing him (the reader) into the story and including him in the action that takes place. The author writes this article as if it were a story and includes the reader in it to make it more relevant. Ask your student's opinion about this style of writing and have him explain why it is or isn't enjoyable or useful.

    To emphasize the writing style, have your student briefly compare and contrast the way this article is written with "Eating Like a Bird" and "The Ocean's Cleaning Stations." You may wish to ask the following questions to guide the discussion:
    - Is each article about one or more than one unusual animal?
    - Which articles give the most information about the animal or animals? Which give the most information about the environment around the animals?
    - How would each article be useful for a research project?

- Which article makes you feel like you are in it? Why? What words and phrases does it use?
- Can you think of a way the articles are alike?
- Can you think of a way they are different?
- Which article is your favorite? Why?

2. Would you like to see a stormflight in person? Why or why not? What details did the author include that influenced your opinion?

5. Activities

It's All in the Details

Review with your student that the *main idea* is the author's main or most important point. Some pieces of writing have an *unstated main idea.* To discover the unstated main idea, the reader must piece together the details the author gives about the topic.

As needed, help your student complete the It's All in the Details page. Use the first three questions, listed below, to focus your student's attention on the termite migration, the main event in the article.

- What is the title of the article?
- What is the main event that takes place in the article?
- Why is that event important to the termites?

Then have your student choose three of the most important details about the stormflight from the article. After he has written them on the page, guide your student to put the unstated main idea in his own words. Responses may vary, but should focus on: After a big storm, termites in West Africa fly out of their mounds to start new colonies.

Answers:

1. The title of the article is "Stormflight."
2. The main event is the termites leaving their mounds after the storm.
3. The event is important because the termites find mates and start new colonies.
4. Accept any reasonable response.
5. Accept any reasonable response.
6. Accept any reasonable response.
7. Accept any reasonable variation on: After a big storm, termites in West Africa fly out of their mounds to start new colonies.

Author's Purpose

Authors have many options when giving their readers information. Why did the author include a box of information at the end of the article? Guide your student to notice the box of information on page 15. Explain that authors have many methods of providing information for the reader. In this case, the article is about the summer stormflight of the termites, and it is written like a story that draws the reader in. But many readers may not know a lot about termites. The box of information provides facts about this subject that may help the reader to understand more about the details in the article.

Have your student read the information in this box and use it to complete the Mighty Termites page. This exercise will help him transfer and reorganize information into an outline. Tell your student that some of the information provided in the box will not be used in the outline.

Lesson 6: "Stormflight": Session 2

Discuss the venues authors have to present information. Write a newspaper article from the information in "Stormflight."

Lesson Notes

This is the second of two sessions on "Stormflight."

Objectives

Demonstrate comprehension of the text.
Identify characteristics of nonfiction.
Compare and contrast characteristics of nonfiction.
Locate and use the table of contents and glossary.
Identify the main idea and details.

Student Pages

"Stormflight": Session 2
Extra! Extra!

Materials

"Stormflight," *Curious Creatures,* pages 12-15

1. Get Ready

Think Ahead

Discuss the following with your student.

1. Summarize the article.
2. How was "Stormflight" like the other articles you read?
3. How was it different?

2. Discuss

Author's Purpose

Remind your student that authors have many ways to present information. Point out that each way serves a specific audience, or group of readers. Discuss with your student the following questions about "Stormflight":

1. What did you like best about the article?
2. What did you notice about the way the article was organized?
3. Now pretend you are writing an article about the termite migration for a newspaper. What do readers expect to find in a newspaper article? What changes would you make to "Stormflight" to make it like a newspaper article? Why?

3. Activity

Extra! Extra! Read All About It!

Have your student rewrite "Stormflight" as a short newspaper article. Point out that people all around the world share information through newspapers and television or radio news reports.

As necessary, help him follow the directions below.

1. Complete the Extra! Extra! page.

   Guide your student to locate facts in the article. Have him explain how the three details he chooses relate to his main idea.

2. Draft the body of your article.

   Have your student review the notes on his Extra! Extra! page and use them to structure and write a draft of a newspaper article. You may wish to have him view other newspaper articles. Remind him of the differences he noted between "Stormflight" and what a newspaper reader expects in a news article. He should write what a newspaper reader would expect to read.

3. Add a hook and a title.

   Have your student write a hook—an interesting lead sentence—to open the article. Hooks often take the form of question and answer, for example, "How can there be plumes of smoke without any fire? It must be a stormflight!" Hooks can also be interesting facts or comparisons, such as, "Last night, the hiss of the storm melted into the buzz of a million new termite wings unfurling for the first time." If your student has difficulty, have him use an article in your local newspaper as a model. Then have him reread his draft and choose a title.

4. Add a pull quote.

   Have your student add a pull quote to his new article. Remind your student that a pull quote is an interesting or surprising sentence that is pulled directly from the article and offset in a bigger typeface. A pull quote is meant to catch the reader's eye and make him want to read the story to learn more.

5. Publish your article! Write and illustrate a neat final copy.

   Remind your student that newspapers use photographs to accompany their articles. His illustration should look as much like a photograph as possible. As necessary, discuss with your student differences between an illustration and a photograph. Compare the illustrations in "Stormflight" with the photos in "Eating Like a Bird" and "The Ocean's Cleaning Stations."

Your student may enjoy pretending he is a television or radio news reporter and reading aloud his article. Encourage him to use simple props, for example, a hairbrush for a microphone or a cardboard box for a television set.

Lesson 7: "A Mom with a Mission": Session 1

Unlike most insects, treehopper females care for and protect their young. Identify the unstated main idea and distinguish between fact and opinion.

Lesson Notes
This is the first of two sessions on "A Mom with a Mission."

Objectives
Demonstrate comprehension of the text.
Classify and categorize details.
Distinguish fact from opinion.
Identify the main idea and details.

Student Pages
"A Mom with a Mission": Session 1
Fact and Opinion

Materials
"A Mom with a Mission," *Curious Creatures*, pages 16-17
1 index card

1. Get Ready

Vocabulary
Have your student use the glossary to look up the definitions to today's vocabulary words.

appendage: (n.)
Humans have four *appendages*: two arms and two legs.

molt: (v.)
When snakes *molt*, they shed their skins.

Tip: You may wish to go over some of the scientific terminology with your student. In this article he will find the terms "species" and "order." Explain that scientists classify living things with shared characteristics into a taxonomy, or a division system that groups organisms by what they look like. A scientist named Carl Linnaeus developed this system in the 1700s.

Scientists divide all living things into five large groups called kingdoms. The five kingdoms are: Plant, Animal, Fungus, Protist (e.g. algae, amoeba), and Moneran (e.g. bacteria).

Within each kingdom there are smaller groupings: Phylum, Class, Order, Family, Genus, and Species. For example, a wolf and a dog are part of the same Kingdom, Phyla, Class, Order, Family, and Genus, but they are of different species. A wolf is Canus lupus and a dog is Canus familiarus. A wolf and a dog are very similar.

Linnaeus gave organisms official Latin names so that people all over the world in the 1700s could use the same names when they talked about living things scientifically. People did not call a dog canus familiarus in regular conversation.

Explain to your student that the italicized Latin words he sees are part of this taxonomy. The treehoppers are part of the order Homoptera and are closely related to other species in that order. The official name for the treehopper is species *Umbonia ataliba*.

Think Ahead

Discuss the following with your student.

1. Look up "A Mom with a Mission" in the table of contents. Look at the illustration. Predict what the article will be about.
2. What do you know about insects?

2. Read

Have your student read "A Mom with a Mission," pages 16-17.

3. Questions

Have your student write the answers to the questions in his Reading Notebook. If he has difficulty, have him read the relevant part of the story aloud.

1. How are treehopper mothers different from most other kinds of insects?
   Treehopper mothers are different from most other kinds of insects because they care for and protect their young.

2. List three things a treehopper does to care for and protect her young.
   Accept any three of the following: She guards the eggs against predators, she stands in front of them or over them, she kicks at predators or spreads her wings to drive them off, and she drills feeding holes for the nymphs.

3. Why are the nymphs camouflaged?
   The camouflage helps them hide from predators.

4. When are the nymphs considered grown up?
   The nymphs are grown up at about six weeks when they molt for the fourth time and can drill their own feeding holes.

5. How many clutches of young does a treehopper raise in her life?
   A treehopper raises one clutch of young in her life.

4. Discuss

Discuss today's reading. If you wish, have your student write a paragraph in response to one of the questions.

1. Why do you think the treehopper works so hard to protect her young?
2. Explain how camouflage and the pronotum help protect the treehoppers.

5. Activities

Discovering the Unstated Main Idea

Remind your student that the main idea is the most important or main point the author makes. An *unstated main idea* is not written out in a sentence. Discuss with your student that a reader must look closely at the details the author gives to discover the unstated main idea.

Have your student write three important details from the article on one side of an index card. You may wish to have him explain why he thinks each detail is important. On the other side of the index card, have him write the main idea in his own words. You may wish to ask him, "What do you think the author most wants you to know about treehoppers?"

Responses will vary, but should focus on: Treehoppers are unusual insects because they care for and guard their young.

Tell him that to double-check that his main idea is correct, he should go back and find at least one more detail in the text that supports the main idea he chose.

Fact and Opinion

Remind your student that nonfiction is writing based on facts. Explain that a fact is a statement that can be proven true. Discuss the following facts with him and have him tell what book he could look in or what he could do to prove each true. Then have him give two more facts and explain how he could prove them true.

- There are seven continents. (You could count them in an atlas, or visit each one.)
- Snails have hard shells. (You could look in a science book, or find one and see.)
- Chocolate is made from cacao nuts. (You could look in an encyclopedia, or visit a chocolate factory!)

Tip: Knowing how to verify information to research a nonfiction article, or where to look to verify information, is an important concept.

Explain that an *opinion* is what a person feels or thinks about something. Opinions are not true or false. People can have different opinions about the same thing without being right or wrong. Have your student look at the opinions below and give his own opinion about the subject. Then have him give two opinions of his own and find out what someone else's opinion is on the same subject. You may also wish to share with him a time when you and a friend or loved one had different opinions about a subject.

- Cherry vanilla is the tastiest flavor of ice cream.
- Salamanders make great pets.
- Green is a pretty color.

Have him complete the Fact and Opinion page. When he finishes, review and discuss his work.

Answers:

1. F	6. F
2. O	7. O
3. O	8. F
4. O	9. C
5. F	10. Accept any reasonable answer.
	11. Accept any reasonable answer.

Lesson 8: "A Mom with a Mission": Session 2

Discuss the author's purpose and design two timelines to illustrate a treehopper's life cycle.

Lesson Notes

This is the second of two sessions on "A Mom with a Mission."

Objectives

Locate and use the table of contents and glossary.

Identify elements of nonfiction.

Classify and categorize details.

Sequence events in a story.

Student Pages

"A Mom with a Mission": Session 2

Life Cycle

Materials

"A Mom with a Mission," *Curious Creatures*, pages 16-17

sheets of plain paper

crayons, markers, or colored pencils

1. Get Ready

Think Ahead

Discuss the following with your student.

Summarize the article. What does a treehopper do that is different from what other insects do?

2. Discuss

Author's Purpose

Explain to your student that authors have many ways to present information. You may wish to brainstorm a list, for example: books, newspaper, encyclopedia, or magazine articles, signs or posters, brochures, websites or computer programs, or fact cards. Point out that each way serves a specific audience, or group of readers. Discuss with your student the following questions about the "A Mom with a Mission" article:

1. What did you like best about the article?
2. What did you notice about the way the article was organized?
3. Pretend you want to learn about the life cycle of a treehopper. What information in the article would you find most useful? What information would you take out? Why?

3. Activities

Treehopper Timeline

Have your student reorganize the information in "A Mom with a Mission" to make a timeline. Point out that a timeline "zooms in" on important events.

As necessary, review the example timeline of a butterfly's life. Explain that on a timeline, events are put in order from the earliest to the most recent. You read timelines from left to right.

Review the article with your student. Then have him turn a piece of paper in a landscape orientation. Have him draw a horizontal line on the paper and write the events listed in the correct order. He may refer to the article as he works.

Answers:

1. The adult female treehopper lays about 90 eggs on the end of a branch.
2. The treehopper mom guards her eggs.
3. The treehopper mom drills feeding holes into the branch.
4. The nymphs move to the feeding holes and start sucking juices.
5. The nymphs are six weeks old. They molt for the fourth time.
6. The adult treehoppers fly away from the branch and find mates.
7. The adult females lay eggs.

Cycle Diagrams

Explain that a *cycle* is a sequence or group of events that is repeated over time. For example, perhaps every day you eat breakfast, then lunch, then dinner. That is a cycle. Encourage your student to think of a cycle of events in his daily routine.

Review the example cycle of a butterfly's life. Discuss how it is similar to and different from the timeline. Guide your student to understand that the events are the same, but the beginning and end of the timeline have been joined. Explain that the cycle begins anew with the next generation of butterflies.

If your student has difficulty understanding the concept of a cycle timeline, draw a nonsensical cycle timeline, for example: Mary learns to walk, Mary loses her first tooth, Mary's seventh birthday, Mary rides a bicycle. Guide your student to see that this timeline does not work as a cycle because the two ends cannot be connected. Ask him: Can Mary learn to walk again after she rides a bicycle? No. Mary moves forward on the timeline. The cycle doesn't begin again.

Have your student complete the Life Cycle page. Remind him that the first and last events in the female treehopper's life cycle must be combined. Guide him to see that the cycle begins anew with the treehopper's young.

He may illustrate his cycle diagram or his timeline.

Lesson 9: "Lingering Leeches"

Leeches are earthworm-like bloodsuckers that have been used for medicinal purposes for the past two thousand years. Discuss fact, opinion, and perspective.

Objectives
Demonstrate comprehension of the text.
Identify characteristics of nonfiction.
Distinguish fact from opinion.
Identify point of view or perspective.
Identify author's style.

Student Pages
"Lingering Leeches"
Is That a Fact?

Materials
"Lingering Leeches," *Curious Creatures*, pages 18-21
2 index cards

1. Get Ready

Vocabulary
Have your student use the glossary to look up the definitions for today's vocabulary words.

> **squeamish:** (adj.) easily nauseated or disgusted
> There is no way I could bait a fishhook with a worm; I am far too *squeamish*.

> **anesthetic:** (n.)
> The doctor gave me an *anesthetic* so I wouldn't feel pain when he gave me stitches.

> **anticoagulant:** (n.)
> *Anticoagulants* are sometimes used to help people with blood clots.

> **secrete:** (v.)
> When you exercise, you *secrete* sweat.

> **transplant:** (n.)
> The patient is on the waiting list for a heart *transplant* because he needs a new heart.

Think Ahead
Discuss the following with your student.

1. Look up "Lingering Leeches" in the table of contents. What does the word *lingering* mean? What clue does that give you about leeches?
2. Look at the illustration. Predict what the article will be about.

2. Read

Have your student read "Lingering Leeches."

3. Questions

Have your student write the answers to the questions in his Reading Notebook. If he has difficulty, have him read the relevant part of the story aloud.

1. Describe two ways leeches use their suckers.
   Leeches use their suckers to move and to suck blood.

2. Why did leech rental help spread diseases?
   Leech rental helped spread diseases because a leech would suck blood out of a person with a disease and then it would get into the blood of the next person who used the leech.

3. How do doctors today sometimes use leeches?
   Doctors today sometimes use leeches to help transplant patients.

4. Why doesn't a leech bite hurt?
   Leech bites don't hurt because leeches secrete an anesthetic when they bite.

4. Discuss

Discuss today's reading. If you wish, have your student write a paragraph in response to one of the questions.

1. There's an old saying that goes, "Too much of anything is no good." How is that true for leeches? Give an example from the article in which leeches helped a person get better, and one in which they didn't.

2. Look at the gray box at the beginning of the article. Read this paragraph again. Why do you think the author chose to begin her article this way? What does this opening paragraph tell you?

   Tip: Guide your student to see that this is another interesting way to begin a piece of nonfiction. If you wish, remind or ask your student how some of the other selections in this unit began.
   - "Eating Like a Bird" compares humans to animals and hooks the reader with a question that suggests the main idea of the article.
   - "The Ocean's Cleaning Stations" reads like an eyewitness report and makes the reader wonder what will happen next.
   - "Stormflight" reads like a story and makes the reader a character in the story by using second person, "you."
   - "A Mom with a Mission" opens with a statement that most readers will agree with: "To us, insects may not seem like the best parents."

Help your student to see that the opening paragraph of "Lingering Leeches" tells a story that many people might identify with and also gives the reader an insight into the author's *opinion* on leeches. Her childhood story suggests that she was afraid of leeches, but another child had a different *perspective,* or *point of view.* Today's lesson will address these concepts.

5. Activities

Is That a Fact?

As necessary, remind your student that a fact is a statement that can be proven true. An opinion is what a person thinks or feels about something.

Remind your student about sources he might use to verify a fact, including the encyclopedia, reference books, authoritative websites, etc.

Have your student complete the Is That a Fact? page. When he finishes, review and discuss his work.

Answers:
1. F
2. O
3. F
4. F
5. F
6. O
7. F
8. F
9. A
10. Accept any reasonable response.
11. Accept any reasonable response.

It All Depends on Your Perspective

Explain to your student that people can know the same facts about something, but have different opinions. Discuss the example: Joe and Cindy both know that it is usually cold in Alaska. Joe loves the cold and snow, so he thinks it would be a nice place to live. Cindy prefers warm climates. She would not like to live in Alaska. Point out to your student that "Alaska is (or is not) a nice place to live" is an opinion, while "Alaska is usually cold" is a fact. Joe and Cindy do not share the same *perspective*.

Review the circumstances of the two children in the article: the author who was a girl in Australia and the boy who was a surgical patient from Boston. Discuss the following questions:

1. What facts do both children know about leeches?
2. What is the girl's opinion of leeches? Find a sentence in the article that supports your answer.
3. What do you think the boy's opinion about leeches would be? Why?

On the lined side of one index card, have your student write a postcard from the girl to the boy, explaining her opinion. On the other index card, have him write a postcard from the boy to the girl, explaining what the boy's opinion would be.

When he finishes, ask him what his opinion is about leeches, and what facts led him to form his opinion and make his decision. Ask him if his opinion changed from when he first began reading the article until he completed this activity. Point out that people's opinions sometimes change when they learn more facts about a subject. You may wish to share a time when your opinion about a subject changed when you learned more about it, or have your student share a similar experience.

Lesson 10: Unit Assessment

Review facts and skills learned and complete the Unit Assessment.

Objectives
Demonstrate comprehension of the text.
Distinguish between fact and opinion.
Identify the main idea and details.
Identify an author's purpose.
Identify author's style.

Materials
Curious Creatures magazine
Bird Watch Brochure
The Ocean's Cleaning Stations Travel Guide
Stormflight Newspaper Article
Treehopper Timeline
Leech Postcards

1. Get Ready

Discuss the following with your student.

1. Review the articles you've read and the projects you've done. Which article was your favorite? Why?
2. How did the author of your favorite article hold your interest? Was it the information or the way the author presented it?
3. What technique did the author use to hook you?

2. Unit Assessment

Before giving the Unit Assessment, take a few minutes to have your student look back at what he has read, the activities he has completed, and the skills he has practiced in his Reading Notebook. Then have him complete the Unit Assessment.

After your student completes the assessment, enter the results online.

Answers:
1. This passage is nonfiction.
2. The passage contains facts and writing about true things. It is not make-believe.
3. A
4. D
5. Accept any reasonable response.
6. Accept any reasonable response.
7. B
8. Accept any reasonable response from the selection.
9. B

10. Accept any reasonable response. Your student should have written his opening as an engaging question, news article, or story. Possible models are below:

Do you think a whale is the biggest fish in the sea?

The great blue whale, nearly 100 feet long, glides gracefully along the waves, surfacing now and again for air.

You are standing on the deck of a ship waiting breathlessly with your binoculars in hand. Suddenly, your long wait is over. You see the great blue whale directly ahead of you. You think it looks as long as a fleet of school buses, and then you learn it is nearly 100 feet in length.

Unit 6: Stories from the Bible

Read stories from the Bible, focusing on character, choices, and consequences. Identify character traits and reasons why characters make difficult decisions.

Lesson 1: "The Story of Ruth"

Ruth has become a symbol of loving dedication and sacrifice for the good of another. Her story shows that caring about others can help a person make a difficult choice and face hardships. Describe the main character and identify choices and consequences in the story.

Lesson Notes

A distinction needs to be made between, on one hand, teaching the Bible as a guide to belief, and, on the other hand, teaching stories from the Bible as literature. Teaching the Bible as a guide to belief is a religious task that belongs to the family (if the family so chooses) or the church. Teaching stories from the Bible as literature—which is the goal of these lessons—is an educational task intended to promote cultural literacy. As E. D. Hirsch, Jr. explains in *The Dictionary of Cultural Literacy* (2nd edition, Boston: Houghton Mifflin, 1993), "No one in the English-speaking world can be considered literate without a basic knowledge of the Bible." Stories, characters, and expressions from the Bible are woven into the fabric of English, in everything from a sportscaster's casual allusion to an uneven match as a "David and Goliath contest" to the poetry of Chaucer, Shakespeare, and Milton.

Objectives

Demonstrate comprehension of the text.
Identify the main events of the plot.
Describe the main character.
Identify choices and consequences.

Student Pages

"The Story of Ruth"
Ruth and Her Choices
Bible Character Chart

Materials

Classics for Young Readers, Vol. 5A, pages 110-114

1. Get Ready

Vocabulary

Go over the vocabulary words with your student before she reads the story.

famine: (n.) a time when there is not enough food for everyone
The year it did not rain, no crops grew, and there was a terrible *famine* in the land.

kindred: (n.) family or relatives
At the family reunion, I met many of my *kindred* whom I had only heard of before.

steadfast: (adj.) firm, unchanging, determined
The brave soldier stood *steadfast* at the gate, ready to guard it against any invaders.

sheaf: (n.) a bundle of grasses or plants that are tied together
We tied the stalks of wheat into *sheaves* and lined them up inside the barn.

Think Ahead
Discuss the following with your student.

Today's story is from the Bible. The main character in the story has to make some very important choices. You make choices every day. Some are small choices, such as choosing what color shirt to wear or what to eat for lunch. But some are big, important choices, such as choosing to tell the truth. Tell about an important choice you have made. Was it hard to make the choice? Why or why not?

Tip: In the Jewish tradition, the book from which this story comes is called the Hebrew Bible; in the Christian tradition, the book is referred to as the Old Testament.

2. Read

Have your student read "The Story of Ruth" in *Classics for Young Readers*, Vol. 5A, pages 110-114.

3. Questions

Have your student write the answers to the questions in her Reading Notebook. If she has difficulty, have her read the relevant part of the story aloud.

1. Why did Naomi want to return to Bethlehem after her husband and sons died?
   Naomi wanted to return to Bethlehem because she had family there and she had heard that there was a good harvest, so she could work and take care of her needs.

2. When she reached Bethlehem, what did Ruth do to take care of Naomi?
   Ruth gleaned in the fields of Boaz to get food for herself and Naomi.

3. Why did Boaz marry Ruth?
   Boaz married Ruth because she was as kind as she was beautiful.

Tip: Guide your student to find the paragraph in which Boaz explained to Ruth why he wanted to help her. He said, "I have been told how you left your father, mother, and the land of your birth, and have come to a strange country to care for your mother-in-law, who is old and alone. May the God of Israel reward you, keep you, and protect you!"

4. Discuss

Discuss today's reading. If you wish, have your student write a paragraph in response to one of the questions.

1. How do you think Ruth felt about leaving her home in Moab and traveling to a strange land?
2. Why do you think Ruth decided to leave her home and do hard work for Naomi's sake?

5. Activities

Choices and Consequences
Tell your student that characters' choices and their consequences are an important part of a story's plot.

For example, recall the childhood story of "The Boy Who Cried Wolf." The shepherd boy chose to lie about the wolf. The consequence was that when the real wolf came and the boy called for help, the villagers did not believe him, and they did not come to his aid.

You may wish to discuss with your student a choice you or she made and its consequences.

As necessary, help your student answer the questions on the Ruth and Her Choices page.

Answers:
1. At the beginning of the story, Naomi was old, poor, alone, and her husband and sons had died.
2. Accept any reasonable answer: Ruth wanted to take care of Naomi; she loved Naomi.
3. When they arrived in Bethlehem, Ruth decided to go to work gleaning in the fields of Boaz.
4. Accept any reasonable answer: Ruth wanted to make sure Naomi had enough food; she didn't want Naomi to have to work; she wanted to take care of Naomi.
5. Ruth brought a bushel of grain back to Naomi, and Boaz fell in love with Ruth.
6. At the end of the story, Naomi went to live with Ruth and Boaz and "was filled with joy."
7. Accept any reasonable answer: Ruth is kind, beautiful, good, caring, compassionate, loyal.

Bible Character Chart
Have your student make an entry on the Bible Character Chart for characters in this unit. On the chart, have her write the following things:

- The main character's name
- The title of the story
- Two or three words or phrases that describe the character
- An important choice the character made
- What mattered most to the character in the story

To help your student understand what the category of "what matters most" is asking for, discuss the following example with your student: In the familiar story of George Washington and the cherry tree, George cared more about telling the truth than not getting into trouble. If your student has difficulty, have her complete this sentence: Ruth cared more about _____ than _____. A reasonable response might be: Ruth cared more about Naomi than about staying in her homeland.

Have your student add Ruth to the chart. Keep this chart for use in future lessons.

Lesson 2: "The Story of David": Session 1

In this story, a young shepherd boy decided to fight for his country. Describe the main character, and identify choices and consequences in the story.

Lesson Notes

A distinction needs to be made between, on one hand, teaching the Bible as a guide to belief, and, on the other hand, teaching stories from the Bible as literature. Teaching the Bible as a guide to belief is a religious task that belongs to the family (if the family so chooses) or the church. Teaching stories from the Bible as literature—which is the goal of these lessons—is an educational task intended to promote cultural literacy. As E. D. Hirsch, Jr. explains in *The Dictionary of Cultural Literacy* (2nd edition, Boston: Houghton Mifflin, 1993), "No one in the English-speaking world can be considered literate without a basic knowledge of the Bible." Stories, characters, and expressions from the Bible are woven into the fabric of English, in everything from a sportscaster's casual allusion to an uneven match as a "David and Goliath contest" to the poetry of Chaucer, Shakespeare, and Milton.

Objectives

Demonstrate comprehension of the text.
Identify the main events of the plot.
Identify choices and consequences.
Describe the main character.

Student Pages

"The Story of David": Session 1
Story Timeline

Materials

Classics for Young Readers, Vol. 5A, pages 115-120

1. Get Ready

Pronunciations

Goliath (guh-LIY-uhth)
Philistine (FIH-luh-steen)

Vocabulary

Go over the vocabulary words with your student before she reads the story.

page: (v.) a helper who takes messages, does errands, and performs other services
"Come, *page*," said the prince to the boy, "and take this message to my father, the king."

defy: (v.) to challenge or dare
The knight *defied* the robber in the castle to come out and do battle.

scarce: (adj.) not plentiful, not much
Food was *scarce* during the famine; most families did not have enough to eat.

pillage: (v.) to rob, to take by force; (n.) something stolen or taken by force
After they raided the village, the band of robbers returned to their hideout to divide their *pillage*.

forage: (v.) to wander in search of food
When their supplies ran out, the explorers had to *forage* in the woods to survive.

upstart: (n.) a person who thinks he is more important than he really is
She is such an *upstart*, she thinks she ought to be first in line for everything.

Think Ahead
Discuss the following with your student.

1. Summarize what you read in "The Story of Ruth."
    Tip: To prepare your student for the assessment at the end of the unit, make sure she includes the following information in her summary:
    *   Ruth's mother-in-law's name (Naomi)
    *   What Ruth did when they reached Bethlehem (she began gleaning in Boaz's fields)
    *   What happened at the end of the story (Ruth and Boaz married and had a son named Obed. Naomi lived in happiness with Ruth, Boaz, and her grandson.)

2. Tell one choice Ruth made and the consequences of that choice.

3. The next Bible story you're going to read tells about the descendants of Ruth and Boaz. (If you don't know the meaning of *descendants,* check a dictionary.)

2. Read

Have your student read "The Story of David" in *Classics for Young Readers*, Vol. 5A, pages 115-120.

3. Questions

Have your student write the answers to the questions in her Reading Notebook. If she has difficulty, have her read the relevant part of the story aloud.

1. At the beginning of the story, why did David go to the palace?
    David went to the palace to play his harp and help make the king well.

2. What people invaded Israel?
    The Philistines invaded Israel.

3. What did the king offer as a reward to the person who killed Goliath?
    To the person who killed Goliath, the king offered a chest of gold, one of his daughters for a wife, and he said he would make the person's father and brothers rulers among the people.

4. Why didn't the king want David to fight Goliath?
    The king didn't want David to fight Goliath because David was only a boy, and Goliath was a man of war.

4. Discuss

Discuss today's reading. If you wish, have your student write a paragraph in response to one of the questions.

1. Describe Goliath. Why didn't any of the Israelite soldiers fight him?
2. David told the king, "Israel's heart should not fail because of a man" (page 119). What do you think David meant?
3. Why did David decide to fight Goliath? What reasons did he give to explain why he should?

5. Activity

Story Timeline

Have your student complete the Story Timeline. As necessary, help her find details in the text.

If needed, explain that to *draw a symbol* means to choose an object that stands for something else. For example, a symbol for the story "Cinderella" might be a glass slipper or a pumpkin coach.

Answers:
1. David was "ruddy-faced, slender, and handsome, with eyes as bright and sharp as an eagle's."
2. David soothed the king by playing music on his harp.
3. Accept any reasonable response.
4. The Philistines attacked Israel while David was at the palace.
5. They made great boasts, but they didn't do anything.
6. Goliath challenged one of the soldiers to fight him. The people who lost would be servants to the people who won.
7. Accept any reasonable response.

Lesson 3: "The Story of David": Session 2

David makes a brave choice to face Goliath in battle. Discuss the consequences of his choice.

Lesson Notes

A distinction needs to be made between, on one hand, teaching the Bible as a guide to belief, and, on the other hand, teaching stories from the Bible as literature. Teaching the Bible as a guide to belief is a religious task that belongs to the family (if the family so chooses) or the church. Teaching stories from the Bible as literature—which is the goal of these lessons—is an educational task intended to promote cultural literacy. As E. D. Hirsch, Jr. explains in *The Dictionary of Cultural Literacy* (2nd edition, Boston: Houghton Mifflin, 1993), "No one in the English-speaking world can be considered literate without a basic knowledge of the Bible." Stories, characters, and expressions from the Bible are woven into the fabric of English, in everything from a sportscaster's casual allusion to an uneven match as a "David and Goliath contest" to the poetry of Chaucer, Shakespeare, and Milton.

Objectives

Demonstrate comprehension of the text.
Identify the main events of the plot.
Identify choices and consequences.
Describe the main character.

Student Pages

"The Story of David": Session 2
Bible Character Chart

Materials

Classics for Young Readers, Vol. 5A, pages 120-122

1. Get Ready

Vocabulary

Go over the vocabulary words with your student before she reads the story.

> **assembly:** (n.) a group of people who come together for a purpose, for example, to make laws, or to worship
> The *assembly* gathered in the council hall to vote for the new mayor.

Think Ahead

Discuss the following with your student.

1. Summarize what you have read so far in the story. In your summary, tell the following things:
   - How David helped the king (He soothed the king by playing his harp.)
   - Who invaded Israel (the Philistines)
   - Who challenged the Israelite army (Goliath)
   - What David decided to do (He decided to fight Goliath.)
2. Do you think David was brave? Do you think he was wise? Why?
3. Predict what you think will happen next, and explain why.

2. Read

Have your student read Chapter 4 in "The Story of David" in *Classics for Young Readers*, Vol. 5A, pages 120-122.

3. Questions

Have your student write the answers to the questions in her Reading Notebook. If she has difficulty, have her read the relevant part of the story aloud.

1. Why didn't David wear the king's armor?
   David didn't wear the king's armor because he couldn't walk in it and had never practiced in it before.

2. What did David take with him to the battle?
   David took a shepherd's staff and sling with him into battle.

3. Copy the sentence in Chapter 4 that tells if David was afraid of Goliath.
   "But David was not at all afraid of him." (Begins at bottom of page 120; remind your student to put quotation marks around the sentence, since she is quoting a passage from the story.)

4. How did David kill Goliath?
   David used his sling to throw a stone at Goliath. The stone hit Goliath in the forehead and he fell down on his face. Then David took Goliath's sword and cut off Goliath's head.

4. Discuss

Discuss today's reading. If you wish, have your student write a paragraph in response to this topic.

What words would you use to describe David? Use evidence from the story to explain why you would choose these words.

5. Activity

Bible Character Chart

Have your student make an entry on the Bible Character Chart for characters in this unit. On the chart, have her write the following things:

- The main character's name
- The title of the story
- Two or three words or phrases that describe the character
- An important choice the character made
- What mattered most to the character in the story

If your student has difficulty with "what matters most," have her complete this sentence: David cared more about _____ than _____. Have your student add David to the chart. Keep this chart for use in future lessons.

Lesson 4: Choices That Count: Session 1

Identify examples of compassion and loyalty in the stories and compare and contrast characters.

Lesson Notes

A distinction needs to be made between, on one hand, teaching the Bible as a guide to belief, and, on the other hand, teaching stories from the Bible as literature. Teaching the Bible as a guide to belief is a religious task that belongs to the family (if the family so chooses) or the church. Teaching stories from the Bible as literature—which is the goal of these lessons—is an educational task intended to promote cultural literacy. As E. D. Hirsch, Jr. explains in *The Dictionary of Cultural Literacy* (2nd edition, Boston: Houghton Mifflin, 1993), "No one in the English-speaking world can be considered literate without a basic knowledge of the Bible." Stories, characters, and expressions from the Bible are woven into the fabric of English, in everything from a sportscaster's casual allusion to an uneven match as a "David and Goliath contest" to the poetry of Chaucer, Shakespeare, and Milton.

Lesson 6 of this unit presents Session 2 of "Choices That Count."

Objectives

Demonstrate comprehension of the text.
Identify the main events of the plot.
Identify choices and consequences.
Compare and contrast characters.

Student Pages

Choices That Count: Session 1
Bible Character Chart
Spotlight on Character (2 pages)

Materials

Classics for Young Readers, Vol. 5A, pages 110-122
poster board
crayons, markers, or colored pencils
index cards

1. Get Ready

Think Ahead

Discuss the following with your student.

1. *Loyalty* means being true to the people, places, and ideas we care about. Describe a time in "The Story of Ruth" or "The Story of David" when a character showed loyalty. (Tip: You might need to prompt your student to articulate David's loyalty to Israel, to his native land and his people.)

2. Loyalty sometimes requires people to put others before themselves. It means doing what's right instead of what's easy. Describe a time in "The Story of Ruth" or "The Story of David" when a character put others before himself or herself.

2. Compare and Contrast Ruth and David

Discuss the following with your student to prepare her to complete the Spotlight on Character project. As necessary, have her go back the Bible Character Chart and the stories in order to find information to support her opinions.

- What did each character do that was brave or difficult? Why did he or she do it?
- Who or what mattered most to each character? Why do you think so?
- How did each character's choice affect others? Did the character make a positive or negative difference in other characters' lives?
- Describe two ways the characters are alike.
- Describe two ways they are different.

3. Spotlight on Character

Have your student use the two Spotlight on Character pages to compare and contrast characters, their choices, and the consequences.

Your student should write the character's name at the top of the page. In the circle at the center of the page, have her draw a picture or a symbol of the character. (As needed, remind her that to *draw a symbol* means to choose an object that stands for something else. For example, a symbol for the story "Cinderella" might be a glass slipper or a pumpkin coach.) Your student can write answers to the questions before or after drawing the picture, whichever she prefers.

In the designated sections on the page, have your student write two or more sentences about each of the four following topics:

1. Tell about the character's important choice.
2. Explain how the character's choice affected other characters.
3. Describe how the character was loyal.
4. Tell what kind of person the character was and why you think so.

Lesson 5: "Daniel in the Lion's Den"

Sometimes it takes great courage to make the right choice. Describe the main character, and identify choices and consequences in the story.

Lesson Notes
A distinction needs to be made between, on one hand, teaching the Bible as a guide to belief, and, on the other hand, teaching stories from the Bible as literature. Teaching the Bible as a guide to belief is a religious task that belongs to the family (if the family so chooses) or the church. Teaching stories from the Bible as literature—which is the goal of these lessons—is an educational task intended to promote cultural literacy. As E. D. Hirsch, Jr. explains in *The Dictionary of Cultural Literacy* (2nd edition, Boston: Houghton Mifflin, 1993), "No one in the English-speaking world can be considered literate without a basic knowledge of the Bible." Stories, characters, and expressions from the Bible are woven into the fabric of English, in everything from a sportscaster's casual allusion to an uneven match as a "David and Goliath contest" to the poetry of Chaucer, Shakespeare, and Milton.

Objectives
Demonstrate comprehension of the text.
Identify the main events of the plot.
Identify choices and consequences.
Describe the main character.

Student Pages
"Daniel in the Lion's Den"
Map of the Persian Empire
Bible Character Chart

Materials
Classics for Young Readers, Vol. 5A, pages 123-126

1. Get Ready

Vocabulary
Go over the vocabulary words with your student before she reads the story.

> **flatter:** (v.) to praise untruthfully or insincerely
> Do you really mean all those compliments or are you just trying to *flatter* me?

> **unwillingly:** (adv.) not wanting to
> When my parents asked me to go to bed in the middle of my favorite movie, I went, but very *unwillingly*.

> **alter:** (v.) to change
> Your drawing is perfect; I would not *alter* a single line.

Think Ahead
Discuss the following with your student.

David helped the Israelites defeat the Philistines. Many years later, in the story you are about to read, Israel was defeated by the Babylonians, and the Babylonians, in turn, by the Persians.

The main character in today's story is Daniel. When he was young, he was captured and taken to the great city called Babylon. The Bible says that, because of his wisdom, Daniel became a trusted advisor to Babylonian and Persian kings.

Have your student look at the map that goes with today's lesson and trace her finger around the Persian Empire. Then have her locate the following:

- Israel and Jerusalem
- Babylon

Tip: The heart of what was once Persia is now the country of Iran. Help your child locate Iran on a world map or globe.

2. Read

Have your student read "Daniel in the Lion's Den" in *Classics for Young Readers*, Vol. 5A, pages 123-126.

3. Questions

Have your student write the answers to the questions in her Reading Notebook. If she has difficulty, have her read the relevant part of the story aloud.

1. Copy one sentence from the story that describes Daniel.
   Accept any reasonable response, for example: "Far from Israel, in the empire of Persia, there lived an old man of such courage and wisdom that he cared only to do right, no matter what the cost."

2. Why were the princes jealous of Daniel?
   The princes were jealous because the king had given Daniel "a place of high honor and great power."

3. Why did the king choose to sign the law?
   The king chose to sign the law because the princes flattered him, and because he was "foolish and vain" and "pleased with this law that would set him even above the gods."

4. What did this law say?
   The law said that no one could pray to any god or ask anything from any man except the king for thirty days. Those who disobeyed would be punished by death.

5. Did Daniel obey the king's law?
   No. Daniel continued praying as he had before.

4. Discuss

Discuss today's reading. If you wish, have your student write a paragraph in response to one of the questions.

1. Did the king want to throw Daniel in the lion's den? Why did he?
2. What explanation did Daniel give for why the lions did not harm him?
3. When Daniel came out of the lion's den, how did he treat the king?

5. Activities

Bible Character Chart
Have your student make an entry on the Bible Character Chart for characters in this unit. On the chart, have her write the following things:

- The main character's name
- The title of the story
- Two or three words or phrases that describe the character
- An important choice the character made
- What mattered most to the character in the story

If your student has difficulty with "what matters most," have her complete this sentence: Daniel cared more about _____ than _____.

Have your student add Daniel to the chart. Keep this chart for use in future lessons

Optional: Seeing Daniel
Have your student describe to you the picture that comes to her mind when she thinks of Daniel in the lion's den. What does she think Daniel is doing? What are the lions doing? Why does she think this?

If your student wants to, have her draw a picture of Daniel in the lion's den. Then supervise her as she goes to the website listed in the online version of this Teacher Guide.

Talk with your student about this painting by the American artist Henry Ossawa Tanner (1859-1937).

Lesson 6: Choices That Count: Session 2

This lesson is OPTIONAL. It is provided for students who seek enrichment or extra practice. You may skip this lesson.

If you choose to skip this lesson, then go to the Plan or Lesson Lists page and mark this lesson "Skipped" in order to proceed to the next lesson in the course.

Prepare for the upcoming unit assessment by reviewing important choices and their consequences.

Lesson Notes

A distinction needs to be made between, on one hand, teaching the Bible as a guide to belief, and, on the other hand, teaching stories from the Bible as literature. Teaching the Bible as a guide to belief is a religious task that belongs to the family (if the family so chooses) or the church. Teaching stories from the Bible as literature—which is the goal of these lessons—is an educational task intended to promote cultural literacy. As E. D. Hirsch, Jr. explains in *The Dictionary of Cultural Literacy* (2nd edition, Boston: Houghton Mifflin, 1993), "No one in the English-speaking world can be considered literate without a basic knowledge of the Bible." Stories, characters, and expressions from the Bible are woven into the fabric of English, in everything from a sportscaster's casual allusion to an uneven match as a "David and Goliath contest" to the poetry of Chaucer, Shakespeare, and Milton.

Objectives

Demonstrate comprehension of the text.
Identify the main events of the plot.
Identify choices and consequences.
Compare and contrast characters.

Student Pages

Choices That Count: Session 2
Choices and Consequences
Bible Character Chart

Materials

Classics for Young Readers, Vol. 5A, pages 110-126

1. Get Ready

Think Ahead

Discuss the following with your student.

Think about Ruth, David, and Daniel. What important choice did each character make?

Tip: Guide your student to understand the following things:
- Ruth had to choose between going with Naomi or staying in her homeland.
- David had to choose between fighting for his country or staying safely out of Goliath's way.
- Daniel had to choose between staying true to his beliefs or following the king's law.

2. Choices and Consequences

Help your student prepare for the unit assessment in the next lesson by having her review important choices and consequences in the three Bible stories.

Have your student complete the Choices and Consequences page. Encourage her to refer to the stories and to her Bible Character Chart pages in order to find passages and details to support her answers.

3. Optional: Seeing Ruth and David

If your student enjoyed the optional activity in the previous lesson (viewing and discussing the painting of Daniel), then go online with her to see how two artists show Ruth and David.

To see a **painting of Ruth and Naomi**, go to the website listed in the online version of this Teacher Guide.

Discuss the painting with your student:
- What point in the story does this painting show?
- What emotion is expressed by the way the artist shows Ruth?

Tip: This painting is by William Blake (1757-1827), an English poet and artist.

To see a **sculpture of David**, go to the website listed in the online version of this Teacher Guide.

Tip: To see close-ups of details of the sculpture, roll your cursor over the words in bold type on this web page.

Discuss the sculpture with your student:
- What point in the story does this sculpture show?
- What words would you use to describe David as this sculpture shows him?

Tip: This sculpture is by Gian Lorenzo Bernini (1596-1680), an Italian sculptor, architect, and painter.

Lesson 7: Unit Assessment: Bible Stories

Have your student take the unit assessment to demonstrate factual knowledge and to write about an important choice.

Lesson Notes

A distinction needs to be made between, on one hand, teaching the Bible as a guide to belief, and, on the other hand, teaching stories from the Bible as literature. Teaching the Bible as a guide to belief is a religious task that belongs to the family (if the family so chooses) or the church. Teaching stories from the Bible as literature—which is the goal of these lessons—is an educational task intended to promote cultural literacy. As E. D. Hirsch, Jr. explains in *The Dictionary of Cultural Literacy* (2nd edition, Boston: Houghton Mifflin, 1993), "No one in the English-speaking world can be considered literate without a basic knowledge of the Bible." Stories, characters, and expressions from the Bible are woven into the fabric of English, in everything from the sportscaster's casual allusion to an uneven match as a "David and Goliath contest" to the poetry of Chaucer, Shakespeare, and Milton.

Objectives

Demonstrate knowledge of major characters, incidents, and terms.
Use facts and details from the story to discuss choices and consequences.

Student Pages

Bible Character Chart
Choices and Consequences pages (from lesson 6)

1. Get Ready

Before giving the unit assessment, take a few minutes to have your student look back at the stories she has read and the activities she has completed, including the Bible Character Chart and the Choices and Consequences pages from the previous lesson.

2. Unit Assessment

Go over the instructions for the Unit Assessment. Once you are sure your student understands what to do in each section, have her complete the assessment on her own.

Part 1: Names and Facts
Answers
1. Naomi
2. Ruth left because Naomi left.
3. In Bethlehem, Ruth gleaned in the fields to help Naomi.
4. Boaz
5. David played music for the king and cheered him.
6. the Philistines
7. Goliath
8. He killed him with a stone hurled from his slingshot.
9. They were jealous because the king put Daniel in a position of great honor and power.

10. They tricked him into signing a law that said that no one could ask anything of, or pray to anyone, except the king for thirty days.
11. He was thrown into the lion's den.
12. He came out of the lion's den unharmed.

Part 2: An Important Choice

Review your student's essay. Did she

- identify a character and describe an important choice the character made?
- explain the consequences of this choice?
- tell whether or not she admires the character for this choice, and why?

Also note whether she used specific facts and details from the story to discuss the points in the first two paragraphs.

3. Unit Assessment: Enter the Results

Be sure to return to the computer and enter the results of the unit assessment.

Unit 7: Early American Lives

Learn about five people whose extraordinary deeds made an impact on early American history. Explore the ways people remember and preserve history, and investigate elements of nonfiction.

Lesson 1: "Young Benjamin Franklin": Session 1

Read about the boyhood of Benjamin Franklin, whom Thomas Jefferson would later call "the greatest man of the age and the country in which he lived."[1] Distinguish between biography and autobiography, and describe a character using evidence from the text.

Lesson Notes
This is the first of two sessions on "Young Benjamin Franklin."

Objectives
Demonstrate comprehension of text.
Identify main events of the plot.
Describe a character using evidence from the text.
Compare and contrast information.
Make inferences and draw conclusions.

Student Pages
"Young Benjamin Franklin": Session 1
Preserving the Past: Biography and Autobiography

Keywords
biography: the story of a person's life
autobiography: the story of a person's life, written by that person

1. Get Ready

Vocabulary
Go over the vocabulary words with your student before he reads the story.

studious: (adj.) paying careful attention to one's learning
The *studious* girl patiently worked on her lessons until she had done them correctly.

calculate: (v.) to solve a problem using math
You need to know the multiplication table to *calculate* the answer to this word problem.

object: (v.) to speak against or strongly disagree
He *objected* to walking across the muddy field because he wanted to keep his new shoes clean.

promptly: (adv.) quickly or immediately
The librarian asked me to return the book *promptly*, because another person was waiting to borrow it.

---

[1] James H. Hutson, "Franklin, Benjamin," *World Book Online Americas Edition*,
     http://www.worldbookonline.com/wbol/wbPage/na/ar/co/209260, June 27, 2002.

endure: (v.) to suffer hardship or misfortune without giving in
Those who *endure* Mount Everest's icy weather and difficult climb are treated to an extraordinary view when they reach the top.

alarmed: (adj.) afraid, worried
I was *alarmed* to hear that it was supposed to rain on the day we planned to have our family picnic.

fatigued: (adj.) tired
After a long day sightseeing, we piled into the car *fatigued*, but content.

inquire: (v.) to ask
After my friend missed two days of soccer practice, I called her to *inquire* about her health..

Think Ahead
Discuss the following with your student.

Today's reading, "Young Benjamin Franklin", begins in the year 1706. In 1706, the United States of America had not yet been formed. Only twelve of the thirteen colonies existed. But great changes were coming, and one little boy in Boston was growing up to become one of the greatest men of that extraordinary time.

As necessary, tell your student:
* Benjamin Franklin lived from 1706-1790. He was an inventor, scientist, statesman, and author. His far-ranging interests and skills earned him Thomas Jefferson's title of "the greatest man of the age and the country in which he lived."[2]
* In 1706, there were only twelve colonies. Georgia was first permanently settled in 1733.
* On July 4th, 1776, the Second Continental Congress adopted the Declaration of Independence, forming the United States of America. The Constitution of the United States was signed on September 17th, 1787.

Tip: You may wish to consult a Benjamin Franklin timeline for an overview of the major events of Franklin's extraordinary life. see www.ushistory.org/franklin/timeline.
For additional information on Benjamin Franklin see www.ushistory.org/franklin.

2. Read

Have your student read Chapters 1-3 of "Young Benjamin Franklin" in *American Lives and Legends*, pages 4-9.

Tip: If you wish, read aloud Chapter 3, "That First Day in Philadelphia" to your student.
If your student enjoys Franklin's autobiography, you may wish additional chapters to him, or allow him to read it independently. It can be found at http://www.ushistory.org/franklin/autobiography/index.htm

---

[2] James H. Hutson, "Franklin, Benjamin," *World Book Online Americas Edition*,
   http://www.worldbookonline.com/wbol/wbPage/na/ar/co/209260, June 27, 2002.

3. Questions

Have your student write the answers to the questions in his Reading Notebook. If he has difficulty, have him read the relevant part of the story aloud.

1. Why did Benjamin's father apprentice him to a printer?

    Benjamin's father apprenticed Benjamin to a printer because Benjamin loved books and reading.

2. Why did Benjamin choose to leave Boston?

    He left Boston because his brother treated him poorly and he could find no other work in Boston.

3. How did Benjamin travel from Boston to Philadelphia?

    Benjamin sailed from Boston to New York, and walked from New York to Philadelphia.

4. Discuss

Discuss today's reading. If you wish, have your student write a paragraph in response to one of the questions.

1. Benjamin Franklin said that going aboard the ship was one of the great *errata* of his life. Why do you think he said that? Do you agree or disagree with him?
2. Describe Benjamin's first day in Philadelphia.

5. Activities

Biography and Autobiography

As necessary, discuss the difference between biography and autobiography with your student. Have him read the examples below, then discuss the questions with him.
*   Benjamin Franklin's parents were poor people who lived in a humble home on Milk Street, and he was the youngest son in the family of seventeen children.
*   I then turned and went down Chestnut Street and part of Walnut Street, eating my roll all the way.

Discuss these questions:
*   Which sentences give facts about Benjamin Franklin's life? [Both sentences give facts about Benjamin's life.]
*   Which sentence comes from Benjamin's biography? How do you know? [The first sentences come from the biography. It talks about him in the third person, and uses *he, him,* and *his* to talk about him.]
*   Which sentence comes from Benjamin's autobiography? How do you know? [The second sentences come from the autobiography. He speaks with his own voice, and uses *I, me,* and *mine.*]
*   Look back at today's reading. Which chapters are a biography? Which are an autobiography? [Chapters 1 and 2 are the biography. Chapter 3 is the autobiography.

Preserving the Past: Biography and Autobiography

In this unit, students will identify ways people remember and preserve history. Guide your student to understand that history is a record of important or significant events for a person, place, or group. Tell your student that one way people remember important events from the past is by writing a biography or an autobiography of a person's life.

Tip: You may wish to discuss reasons why people study and remember history.

Have your student find important facts in the text for the Preserving the Past: Biography and Autobiography page. Encourage him to find more than five facts, and then select the facts that are the most important. Next, have him make inferences about Benjamin Franklin using facts from the story.

Answers:

Facts: Accept any reasonable facts, for example: Benjamin Franklin was the youngest son in a family of seventeen children, or when he was little, Benjamin Franklin wished to be a sailor.

1. Accept any reasonable answer, for example: Benjamin Franklin was determined because he walked all the way from New York to Pennsylvania.
2. Accept any reasonable answer, for example: Learning was important to Benjamin Franklin. He read all the books he could get a hold of.

Lesson 2: "Young Benjamin Franklin": Session 2

Learn about Franklin's adulthood, discuss one of his proverbs from *Poor Richard's Almanac*, and describe one of his accomplishments.

Lesson Notes

This is the second of two sessions on "Young Benjamin Franklin." Your student will need to do additional research for the "More Facts about Franklin" activity. You will need to save the Important Places in American History map for use in future lessons.

Objectives

Demonstrate comprehension of text.
Identify main events of the plot.

Student Pages

"Young Benjamin Franklin": Session 2
Important Places in American History map
Ordinary People, Extraordinary Lives

Materials

optional: encyclopedia
optional: Internet resources

1. Get Ready

Vocabulary

Go over the vocabulary words with your student before he reads the story.

squander: (v.) to spend foolishly or waste
I *squandered* most of my allowance on treats, so I did not have enough money to buy the paints I wanted.

dissatisfied: (adj.) not happy, not pleased
He liked the head and the body of the shark he drew, but he was *dissatisfied* with the tail.

proprietor: (n.) owner
Jack loved books and reading so much that when he grew up, he became the *proprietor* of a bookstore.

coaxingly: (adv.) in a flattering or persuasive way
She called *coaxingly* to the kitten, hoping it would come and sit on her lap.

grave: (adj.) serious
Their faces were *grave* as they discussed the rules.

crestfallen: (adj.) ashamed, disappointed
I was *crestfallen* when I wasn't chosen for the team.

Think Ahead

Discuss the following with your student.

1. Summarize the chapters from "Young Benjamin Franklin."

    Tip: To prepare your student for the assessment at the end of the unit, make sure he includes the following information about Franklin in his summary:

    - Where he grew up (Boston)
    - The trade he learned (he learned to be a printer)
    - The city he moved to (Philadelphia)

2. What words would you use to describe Benjamin Franklin? Why?

    Accept any reasonable response, for example: he was studious because he read and studied with great care, or he was brave and determined because he made the journey from Boston to Philadelphia alone.

2. Read

Have your student read Chapters 4-5 of "Young Benjamin Franklin" in *American Lives and Legends*, pages 9-12.

3. Questions

Have your student write the answers to the questions in his Reading Notebook. If he has difficulty, have him read the relevant part of the story aloud.

1. What is an *almanac?*

    An almanac is a book that contains calendars, recipes, and predictions about the weather that is published once a year.

2. Who is the author of *Poor Richard's Almanac?*

    Benjamin Franklin was the author of *Poor Richard's Almanac.*

3. What name did he use when he published the almanac?

    Benjamin Franklin used the name Richard Saunders when he published the almanac.

4. Discuss

Discuss today's reading. If you wish, have your student write a paragraph in response to one of the questions.

1. In your own words, explain why Benjamin Franklin continued to raise the price of the book that the man in his print shop was trying to buy.

    Guide your student to see that Franklin was frustrated because the man was wasting his time. He continued to raise the price in the hope that the man would see this.

2. A proverb is a brief, popular saying that contains a familiar truth, or useful thought. Find the proverb in Chapter 4. What does it mean? Do you agree or disagree? Why?

> Guide your student to see that the proverb in the selection is at the bottom of the story: "He who squanders his own time is foolish and he who wastes the time of others is a thief." Ask your student what he thinks of wasting other people's time.

3. Choose one proverb from *Poor Richard's Almanac.* What does it mean? Is it good advice? Why?

> Tip: Your student may enjoy exploring more of Franklin's proverbs. See www.ushistory.org/franklin/quotable.

5. Activities

More Facts about Franklin

Have your student do research to find the answers that complete the sentences below. When he finishes, have him copy the sentences into his Reading Notebook, and add one more interesting fact he learned in his research. He will then use these sentences to help him create a symbol for Franklin and add it to the Important Places in American History map.

You may wish to suggest the following resource for research: www.ushistory.org/franklin (or use an encyclopedia).

1. Benjamin Franklin was an author, but he was also a scientist, an inventor, and a statesman. Research the answers to the following questions and then write the completed sentences in your Reading Notebook. Add one more interesting fact that you learn as you read.

> Benjamin Franklin was one of the first people to experiment with _(electricity)_ . He flew a _(kite)_ during a thunderstorm, and proved that lightning was a kind of electricity. He invented the _(lightning rod)_ , which saved his and many other people's homes from being damaged when they were struck by lightning.

> Benjamin Franklin helped write the _(Declaration of Independence)_ , which made the United States of America its own country. He was the oldest person who signed it.

2. Look at the Important Places in American History map. Write the number of the sentence that describes Benjamin Franklin beside Philadelphia, the city in which he lived.

> Sentence number 4 describes Franklin.

3. In what colony (now a state) is Philadelphia?

> Philadelphia is in Pennsylvania.

4. Use the facts you have learned about Franklin to help you create a symbol for the man or one of his accomplishments. Draw a symbol in the box to represent Benjamin Franklin.

> Remind your student that to draw a symbol means to choose an object that stands for something else. For example, a symbol for the story "Cinderella" might be a glass slipper or a pumpkin coach. A symbol for Benjamin Franklin might be a book or a representation of one of his proverbs, such as a penny for "A penny saved is a penny earned." Other symbols might be a lightning bolt or kite to represent Franklin's experiment with electricity.

Ordinary People, Extraordinary Lives

Have your student complete an Ordinary People, Extraordinary Lives page for each person in the unit.

Have your student write the person's name and main area where he or she lived on the lines provided. Then have him write a paragraph that explains one thing the person did that was extraordinary and at least one reason why it was extraordinary. Remind him to write as if his reader has not read the story.

If he would like to draw a picture of the person, encourage him to do so. You may also wish to have him research and add the dates of the person's life.

Save this page, as it will be used for review and writing activities later in this unit.

Lesson 3: "Phillis Wheatley: A Poem to King George"

Meet Phillis Wheatley, a woman who began her life in America as a slave, but became the first published African-American poet. Discuss her poem, and write about one of her extraordinary accomplishments.

Objectives
Demonstrate comprehension of text.
Identify main events of the plot.
Identify author's purpose.

Student Pages
"Phillis Wheatley: A Poem to King George"
Ordinary People, Extraordinary Lives
Important Places in American History

1. Get Ready

Vocabulary
Go over the vocabulary words with your student before he reads the story.

crossly: (adv.) in a bad-tempered way
"Stop pulling my ponytail," she said *crossly,* "I don't like it."

repeal: (v.) to undo or unmake a law
President Abraham Lincoln helped *repeal* the laws that allowed slavery in the United States.

seldom: (adj.) rarely, not often
We *seldom* go to the zoo, perhaps only once or twice each year.

feebly: (adv.) weakly
The newborn kitten *feebly* struggled to its feet and took its first steps.

gilded: (adj.) having a thin covering of gold
That picture frame is not solid gold, it is made of wood that has been *gilded.*

meanest: (adj.) having few means; poor
It broke my heart to think that the poor family in the story lived in the *meanest* little hovel in the village.

clime: (n.) a poetic term meaning climate or region of the earth
Tim enjoys the sun and hot weather, so he chooses to vacation in tropical *climes.*

Think Ahead
Discuss the following with your student.

Today's reading tells the story of a little girl who faced challenges that most people today cannot begin to understand. Yet, she rose above the difficulties and accomplished great things. As you read her story, think about her circumstances as well as her extraordinary talent. You may wish to discuss slavery in America and the lives that most slaves led. Phillis Wheatley's living situation with the Wheatley family was unusual for the time. You may wish to discuss this with your student; however, you will want to stress that Phillis still had great obstacles to overcome to become a published writer.

Tip: You may wish to explain the following to your student before reading:
- The British Parliament passed the Stamp Act in 1765 to raise money to pay for the British soldiers stationed in the United States. Many colonists opposed the Stamp Act. They argued that taxes could not be collected unless the people being taxed (in this case, the colonists) agreed to it, giving rise to the famous slogan, "No taxation without representation." The British Parliament repealed the Stamp Act in 1766.
- The Sons of Liberty were groups of colonists who actively supported American independence before and during the Revolutionary War.

2. Read

Have your student read "Phillis Wheatley: A Poem to King George" in *American Lives and Legends*, pages 13-20.

Tip: You may wish to read the poem "To the King's Most Excellent Majesty" (p. 20) aloud to your student.

3. Questions

Have your student write the answers to the questions in his Reading Notebook. If he has difficulty, have him read the relevant part of the story aloud.

1. How did Phillis come to live with the Wheatley family?
   Phillis was bought as a slave for the Wheatley family.

2. Name two things the Wheatley family taught Phillis how to do.
   Accept any reasonable response, for example: They taught her to read and write in English and in Latin.

3. Why did Phillis write the poem to King George?
   Phillis wrote the poem because she wanted King George to know how happy the people were that he had repealed the Stamp Act.

4. What was Phillis Wheatley the first African-American to do?
   Phillis Wheatley was the first African-American to have a book of poetry published.

5. In the story, Samuel Adams tells Phillis Wheatley, "You have a great gift ... a very great gift, and it must be used." What do you think he meant? Do you think Phillis Wheatley used her gift?
   Accept any reasonable response. Guide your student to see that Phillis Wheatley's many poems are a demonstration of her gift.

4. Discuss

Discuss the following questions to prepare your student to read Henry Wadsworth Longfellow's narrative poem, "Paul Revere's Ride," in the next lesson.

Remind your student that history is the story of what happened to a person, place, or group. One way people preserve history is to write biographies and autobiographies. Another way to remember an important event is to memorialize it in a song or poem. As necessary, review the lyrics of "The Star

Spangled Banner" or "My Country, Tis of Thee" with your student, and discuss the event or events the song tells about.

1. Who was the poem for?
   King George
   Tip: Point out that Phillis Wheatley wrote her poem to commemorate, or remember, an important event.

2. What important event did Phillis Wheatley write about?
   The repeal of the Stamp Act

3. How did the colonists feel about the event? How do you know?
   They were overjoyed; they decorated the Liberty Tree and celebrated.

4. Why did Phillis Wheatley write the poem?
   She wrote it to tell the king about how the colonists felt.

5. How is the language in the poem different from the language you usually use or see? Why do you think she wrote it that way?
   Accept any reasonable response, for example: The language is more formal and more difficult. She wrote it that way because she was talking about something important to her and because she was writing to the king.

5. Activities

Ordinary People, Extraordinary Lives

Have your student complete an "Ordinary People, Extraordinary Lives" page for Phillis Wheatley. As necessary, guide your student to write on the lines Phillis's name and the place where she lived. Then instruct him to write a paragraph that tells about one of Phillis Wheatley's extraordinary accomplishments. Remind your student to give at least one reason why the accomplishment was extraordinary. If your student wishes, he may draw a picture.

Save this page, as it will be used for review and writing activities later in this unit.

Important Places in American History

Have your student add Phillis Wheatley to his Important Places in American History map.

1. Look at the Important Places in American History map. Write the number of the sentence that describes Phillis Wheatley beside Boston, the city in which she lived.
   As needed guide your student to recognize that sentence 2 describes Phillis Wheatley.

2. In what colony (now a state) was Boston located?
   Boston is in Massachusetts.

3. Draw a symbol in the box to represent Phillis Wheatley.
   Remind your student that to draw a symbol means to choose an object that stands for something else. For example, a symbol for the story "Cinderella" might be a glass slipper or a pumpkin coach. A symbol for Phillis Wheatley might be a quill pen to represent her writing.

Lesson 4: "Paul Revere's Ride"

Ride along with Paul Revere in Henry Wadsworth Longfellow's famous poem. Identify and describe the main events of the plot.

Lesson Notes
Henry Wadsworth Longfellow was an American poet who lived from 1807-1882. He was the most popular poet of his time. In "Paul Revere's Ride," Longfellow makes a historical error: Paul Revere never reached Concord. The British captured him and the two other riders, William Dawes and Samuel Prescott, outside of Lexington. Prescott was the only rider to reach Concord.

Objectives
Demonstrate comprehension of text.
Identify main events of the plot.
Identify author's purpose.

Student Pages
"Paul Revere's Ride"
"Paul Revere's Ride" Storyboard

Materials
crayons, markers, or colored pencils

1. Get Ready

Vocabulary
Go over the vocabulary words with your student before he reads the story.

belfry: (n.) a room that houses a bell
We climbed a hundred stairs to the *belfry* at the top of the tower to see the ancient bell.

muffled: (adj.) quieted
The sound of her voice was *muffled* by the heavy scarf she wore.

spar: (n.) a strong pole used to hold sails and ropes on ships
The sailor carefully checked the *spar* for cracks that might make it too weak to hold the sails and rigging.

hulk: (n.) a heavy, clumsy ship
The *hulk* rolled and dipped in the water like a lazy whale.

muster: (n.) a group
A *muster* of soldiers gathered at the fort to prepare for battle.

tread: (n.) the sound or act of walking
The puppy sat by the door, listening for the sound of its master's heavy *tread* on the stair.

grenadier: (n.) a soldier who carries or throws grenades
The *grenadier* checked his grenades and tucked them safely into his pack.

impetuous: (adj.) excited, impatient
The *impetuous* young explorer charged into the jungle, leaving the rest of his party far behind.

linger: (v.) to be slow in leaving
The moon seemed to *linger* over the lake, as if gazing upon her reflection in the water.

kindled: (v.) to have started a fire
She *kindled* a fire by rubbing two sticks together.

Think Ahead

Discuss the following with your student.

1. In the last story you read Phillis Wheatley's poem to King George. Why did Phillis write that poem?
    As necessary, remind your student that Wheatley wrote that poem to honor King George.

2. Can you think of other famous poems or songs that commemorate important events or celebrate the lives of important people? In this lesson, you'll read one about famous American, Paul Revere.

    Tip: You may wish to tell your student that Paul Revere was a patriot who lived from 1734–1818. He carried messages between different patriot groups. In 1773 he spread the word about the Boston Tea Party to New York and Philadelphia. In 1774 he again rode to Philadelphia to spread the news that the British had closed Boston Harbor.

    On the evening of April 18, 1775, Paul Revere was sent Lexington, Massachusetts, to warn Samuel Adams and John Hancock that British troops were marching to arrest them. On the way to Lexington, Revere "alarmed" the countryside, stopping at each house, and arrived in Lexington about midnight. He did not, contrary to popular belief, shout "The British are coming." This would have confused people because many colonists still considered themselves to be British. He told the people that the Regulars (the British soldiers) were on their way. Revere never made it to Concord, he and his companions were stopped after leaving Lexington.

    Poet Henry Wadsworth Longfellow celebrated these accomplishments in the poem your student will read in today's lesson.

2. Read

Have your student read "Paul Revere's Ride" in *American Lives and Legends*, pages 21-26.

3. Questions

Have your student write the answers to the questions in his Reading Notebook. If he has difficulty, have him read the relevant part of the story aloud.

1. Why did Paul Revere ride to the villages and farms?
    Paul Revere rode to the villages and farms to warn the people that the British were coming.

2. Did the British come by land or by sea?
    The British soldiers came by sea.

3. How did Paul Revere know that?

    Paul Revere knew because his friend lit two lamps in the belfry.

    Tip: Guide your student to the following lines. Read them aloud if needed.

    > And lo! As he looks, on the belfry's height
    > A glimmer, and then a gleam of light!
    > He springs to the saddle, the bridle he turns,
    > But lingers and gazes, till full on his sight
    > A second lamp in the belfry burns!

4. On what date did Paul Revere and the two other patriots make their famous ride?

    They made their ride on April 18, 1775.

    Tip: You may wish to tell your student that April 18, 1775, was the day before the fighting broke out at Lexington and the Revolutionary War began.

5. To what towns does Paul Revere ride?

    The poem states that Paul Revere rides through Medford, Lexington, and Concord. As necessary, help your student to find the names of these towns in the eighth, ninth and tenth stanzas of the poem. Then remind your student that, historically, Revere never reached Concord.

4. Discuss

Discuss today's reading. If you wish, have your student write a paragraph in response to one of the questions.

1. Because Paul Revere warned the colonists, when the British soldiers arrived, the colonists were ready to give battle. And that battle, the Battle of Lexington and Concord, began the Revolutionary War. What might have happened if the colonists had not been warned? How might history have been different?

2. Reread the last five lines of the poem. Do you think the poet meant that people can still hear Paul Revere's horse? What do you think he meant?

5. Activities

A Narrative Poem

Tell your student that a narrative poem is a poem that tells a story. Have your student read aloud and then summarize the following stanzas:

1. He said to his friend, "If the British march
    By land or sea from the town tonight,
    Hang a lantern aloft in the belfry arch
    Of the North Church as a signal light –
    One if by land, and two if by sea;
    And I on the opposite shore will be,
    Ready to ride and spread the alarm
    Through every Middlesex village and farm,
    For the country folk to be up and to arm."

2. It was twelve by the village clock
   When he crossed the bridge into Medford town.
   He heard the crowing of the cock,
   And the barking of the farmer's dog,
   And felt the damp of the river fog,
   That rises after the sun goes down.

Sample summary 1:
Paul Revere told his friend to hang one light in the belfry if the soldiers were coming by land, and two if they were coming by sea. He said that he would be on the opposite shore, ready to ride and warn the colonists.

Sample summary 2:
Paul Revere arrived in Medford at midnight. A rooster crowed, a dog barked, and it was foggy.

When he finishes, have him use the Paul Revere's Ride Storyboard to retell the main events in the poem. You may have him identify, put in order, and illustrate the main events on his own. You may also wish to provide him with a list of scrambled main events (such as the one below) and have your student look back to the poem to put the events in order and find details for his illustrations.

Sample list of main events and order:
- Paul Revere rides into Medford to warn the people. (4)
- The British ship, *Somerset,* sails across the bay. (2)
- Paul Revere and his friend decide on the signal. (1)
- Paul Revere rides into Lexington. (5)
- Paul Revere sees two lights in the belfry. (3)
- Paul Revere rides into Concord. (6)

Lesson 5: Words to Remember: "Paul Revere's Ride"

Examine and perform part of Longfellow's poem, "Paul Revere's Ride."

Objectives
Demonstrate comprehension of text.
Identify main events of the plot.
Identify imagery.
Plan and perform readings of selected texts using clear diction and voice quality appropriate to the selection.

Student Pages
Words to Remember: "Paul Revere's Ride"
Ordinary People, Extraordinary Lives

Materials
crayons, markers, or colored pencils

Keywords
imagery: language that appeals to the senses and creates a mental picture that makes readers see, hear, smell, taste, or feel things in their imagination

1. Get Ready

Think Ahead
Have your student use his Paul Revere's Ride Storyboard to complete an Ordinary People, Extraordinary Lives page for Paul Revere. As necessary, guide your student to write Revere's name and the second town he rode to (Lexington) on the lines. He should then write a paragraph that tells about one of Revere's extraordinary accomplishments, and, if he wishes, draw a picture. Remind your student to give at least one reason why the accomplishment was extraordinary.

Save this page, as it will be used for review and writing activities later in this unit.

2. Discuss

Rhythm and Verse
Discuss imagery and rhythm with your student to prepare him to perform a stanza from "Paul Revere's Ride" in the following activity.

Tell your student that Longfellow's poem contains both facts and *imagery.* Imagery is language that appeals to the senses and creates a mental picture. Imagery makes readers see, hear, smell, taste, or feel things in their imagination.

Tip: You may wish to discuss with your student a few short examples of imagery, for example: "the coal-black night," "the stinging cold," "the rapping and tapping of rain on the roof."

Discuss the following example and the questions below. The goal of the discussion is for the student to understand that while facts objectively tell what happened, imagery can influence our thoughts and feelings about a subject.

Example: Longfellow could have written the fact, "The British ship was called the *Somerset.*" Instead, he used this imagery:

> Where swinging wide at her mooring lay
> The *Somerset,* British man-of-war;
> A phantom ship, with each mast and spar
> Across the moon like a prison bar

1. What do phrases like "phantom ship" and "prison bar" make you think of?
    > Answers will vary but may include: ghosts, being put in jail, things that are scary or dangerous.

2. What words and feelings describe the picture you see when you imagine the *Somerset*'s masts and rigging covering the moon like prison bars?
    > Answers will vary but may include: fear, suspicion, danger, a feeling of being threatened

3. Think about the imagery Longfellow used to describe the ship. Why do you think he describes the ship in this way?
    > Guide your student to see Longfellow is creating a tense mood. He wants to show how threatening the British were and reinforce Revere's heroism.

4. What different words or feelings might you think of if Longfellow had described the *Somerset* this way:
    > Where swinging wide at her mooring lay
    > The *Somerset,* British man-of-war;
    > A <u>steadfast</u> ship, with each mast and spar
    > <u>Cradling</u> the moon <u>like a mother's arm</u>

    > Answers will vary but may include: Words like steadfast, cradling, and mother's arm call to mind images of loyalty, love, and trust. It might make a reader feel like the ship and the soldiers are a protective presence rather than a threat. You may wish to explain to your child that people who wanted England to win the Revolutionary War might have chosen those words to describe the Somerset.

Have your student find another example of imagery in the poem. If he has difficulty, have him focus on Stanzas 4 and 5, which include:

*   eager ears (stanza 4, line 2)

*   trembling ladder (stanza 4, line 14)

*   He could hear, like a sentinel's tread
    The watchful night-wind, as it went,
    Creeping along from tent to tent,
    and seeming to whisper, "All is well!" (stanza 5, lines 4-7)

*   A line of black that bends and floats
    On the rising tide, like a bridge of boats (stanza 5, lines 14-15)

Explain to your student that the rhythm of a poem can enhance or contribute to its imagery. Have your student choose and read aloud his favorite stanza. Then discuss the following questions to direct your student's attention to the rhythm of the poem, what images it brings to mind, and why Longfellow might have used it as a poetic device.

- What does the rhythm remind you of: hoof beats, waves lapping against the side of a boat, or something else?
- Why do you think Longfellow wrote the poem in this rhythm?

3. Activity

Preserving the Past: Performance

Explain to your student that some people keep history alive by reciting poems, acting out plays, or taking part in re-enactments by dressing up as and acting like historical figures.

Tip: You may wish to have your student research Ralph Archbold, a Benjamin Franklin portrayer in Philadelphia, Pennsylvania, or the outdoor museum at Colonial Williamsburg in Williamsburg, Virginia.

Then have your student read aloud or act out his favorite stanza from "Paul Revere's Ride."

1. Review the stanza with your student. Have him summarize the stanza in his own words, look for imagery, and help him decide how to say his lines. You may wish to prompt him with such questions as:
    - How might you say words like "phantom ship" to help the audience feel the threat to the colonists that the British ship and soldiers posed?
    - How would you read a line like "Now soft on the sand, now loud on the ledge" to reflect the soft sound on the sand and the loud sound on the rocks?

2. As needed, remind your student that to *rehearse* means to practice in preparation for a performance. Provide constructive criticism as your student rehearses his lines. Encourage him to read clearly and enunciate each word. Practice the lines with him as necessary, and praise him for efforts at expressive reading. If he wishes, he may gather props and a costume for his performance. Encourage him to research what people from Paul Revere's time wore and carried.

    Tip: Sit at a distance from your student, as though you were in the audience. Is he speaking loudly and clearly enough for you to understand him? Encourage him to project his voice so he can be heard and understood.

3. As needed, help your student prepare a brief summary of the stanzas he will not be performing to share with the audience. He should briefly identify the most important events.

Invite family and friends to view the performance. Have your student deliver a brief summary of what has happened so far in the poem. If he acts out a stanza that ends before the end of the poem, then after he reads aloud or acts out his stanza, have him summarize the remainder of the poem as well.

Lesson 6: "Sybil Ludington: The Female Paul Revere"

Like Paul Revere, 16-year-old Sybil Ludington rode through the night to muster American soldiers for a battle with the British. Identify, describe, and design a monument or memorial to commemorate her ride.

Objectives
Demonstrate comprehension of text.
Identify main events of the plot.

Student Pages
"Sybil Ludington: The Female Paul Revere"
Important Places in American History
Ordinary People, Extraordinary Lives
Preserving the Past: Monuments and Memorials

Materials
crayons, markers, or colored pencils

1. Get Ready

Vocabulary
Go over the vocabulary words with your student before he reads the story.

tactic: (n.) a way to accomplish something
My little sister seems to have a million *tactics* for staying up past her bedtime.

urgently: (adv.) needing immediate attention
"Doctor, come quickly," he said *urgently*, "my father is very ill."

intently: (adv.) with great concentration
She looked *intently* at the pieces of the jigsaw puzzle, trying to decide how they fit together.

raid: (n.) an attack
The enemy soldiers led a *raid* upon the village, and burned all the buildings and fields to the ground.

muster: (v.) to cause to gather
We're going to play a pick-up game of ball in the park if I can *muster* enough players to form two teams.

brigands: (n.) thieves, highwaymen
The *brigands* hid in the woods and robbed the carriages that passed by.

plunder: (v.) to steal or take something by force
The pirates *plundered* the merchant ship, carrying away everything that wasn't nailed down.

notorious: (adj.) generally known and talked of in an unfavorable way
The group waited impatiently for Martha, who was *notorious* for being late.

Think Ahead
In the last two lessons, you read about Paul Revere's famous midnight ride. In today's lesson, you will read about another Revolutionary-era messenger. Before you do, add Paul Revere to your map.

1. Look at the Important Places in American History map. Write the number of the sentence that describes Paul Revere beside Lexington, one of the cities he rode to.

    As necessary, guide your student to match sentence 1 with Paul Revere.

2. In what colony (now a state) was Lexington located?

    Lexington is in the state of Massachusetts.

3. Draw a symbol in the box to represent Paul Revere.

    Remind your student that that to draw a symbol means to choose an object that stands for something else. For example, a symbol for the story "Cinderella" might be a glass slipper or a pumpkin coach. A symbol for Paul Revere might be two lights in a belfry.

4. Today's reading begins in the spring of 1777, two years after Paul Revere's famous ride. America has declared its independence from England. The Revolutionary War has begun. General George Washington, the Commander in Chief of the American soldiers, has allowed the men to go home and do their spring planting. But will the British wait? Read on and find out!

    As necessary, tell your student:
    - America declared its independence from England in the Declaration of Independence, adopted by the Second Continental Congress on July 4, 1776.
    - The Revolutionary War began on April 19, 1775, when British soldiers and Americans fought outside of Lexington and Concord following Paul Revere's ride.
    - George Washington was elected Commander in Chief of the American soldiers on June 15, 1775. He was elected President in February 1789.
    - "Spring planting"' is the time when farmers sow the seeds they wish to grow for the season.

2. Read

Have your student read "Sybil Ludington: The Female Paul Revere" in *American Lives and Legends*, pages 27-31.

3. Questions

Have your student write the answers to the questions in his Reading Notebook. If he has difficulty, have him read the relevant part of the story aloud.

1. Why had many of the American troops gone home from the war?

    Many of the American troops had gone home to do their spring planting.

2. After listening to the messenger, what was Colonel Ludington afraid would happen?

    Colonel Ludington was afraid that the British would attack the county.

3. Why couldn't the messenger ride to warn the people of the farms and villages?

    The messenger couldn't ride because he was exhausted.

4. Who rode in the messenger's place?

    Sybil Ludington rode in the messenger's place.

4. Discuss

Discuss today's reading. If you wish, have your student write a paragraph in response to one of the questions.

1. Why was Sybil Ludington's ride dangerous? Why do you think she did it?
2. Why was her ride important? Give two or more reasons.

5. Activities

Ordinary People, Extraordinary Lives

Have your student complete an "Ordinary People, Extraordinary Lives" page for each historical figure. As necessary, guide your student to write each person's name and the place where he or she lived on the lines, write a paragraph that tells the person's extraordinary accomplishment, and, if he wishes, draw a picture. Remind your student to give two or more reasons in support of his opinion.

Save this page, as it will be used for review and writing activities later in this unit.

Preserving the Past: Monuments and Memorials

As necessary, explain to your student that a memorial is something made to remember a person or event, and a monument is a stone or building erected to commemorate the same. You may wish to tell your student that memorials can include statues, sculpture, or a specific area of land.

Have your student research three or more monuments or memorials in the United States, discuss how they are alike or different, and, where appropriate, talk about how and why each was created. Suggested monuments and memorials, listed in alphabetical order, include, but are not limited to:
- The Franklin Delano Roosevelt Memorial
- The Jefferson Memorial
- The Korean War Veterans Memorial
- The Lincoln Memorial
- Mount Rushmore National Memorial
- The USS Arizona Memorial
- The Vietnam Veterans Memorial
- The Washington Monument

You may also wish to have your student research the history of local monuments and memorials.

When he finishes, have him design a monument or memorial to Sybil Ludington on the Preserving the Past: Monuments and Memorials page. As necessary, guide him to explain why he chose his design and what it represents.

Lesson 7: "Sequoyah's Great Invention"

The Cherokee did not have a way to write their language until the early 1800s when Sequoyah, with single-minded dedication, invented a writing system for the Cherokee language.

Objectives
Demonstrate comprehension of text.
Identify main events of the plot.
Compare and contrast information.

Student Pages
"Sequoyah's Great Invention"
Important Places in American History
Ordinary People, Extraordinary Lives: Benjamin Franklin, Phillis Wheatley, Paul Revere, Sybil Ludington
Ordinary People, Extraordinary Lives: Sequoyah

Materials
crayons, markers, or colored pencils
stapler

1. Get Ready

Vocabulary
Go over the vocabulary words with your student before he reads the story.

> **fascinated:** (adj.) very interested, to feel wonder
> My brother was so *fascinated* by the space shuttle exhibit at the museum that he stayed there long after the rest of us had gone to look at the other exhibits.

> **devote:** (v.) to give a certain amount of time and effort to accomplishing something
> I want to be a ballet dancer when I grow up, so I *devote* at least one hour each day to stretching and practicing.

Think Ahead
Discuss the following with your student.

1. Look at the Important Places in American History map. Write the number of the sentence that describes Sybil Ludington beside Putnam County, the place where she lived.
    As necessary, guide your student to match sentence 3 with Sybil Ludington.

2. In what colony (now a state) was Putnam County located?
    Putnam County is in the state of New York.

3. Draw a symbol in the box to represent Sybil Ludington.
    Remind your student that that to draw a symbol means to choose an object that stands for something else. For example, a symbol for the story "Cinderella" might be a glass slipper or a pumpkin coach. A symbol for Sybil Ludington might be a horse.

4. Today you'll read about a man who was a Cherokee Indian. The Cherokee lived in the southeastern part of the United States, on the land that is now Tennessee, North Carolina, South Carolina, Georgia, and Alabama. Find these states on a map.

   As necessary, tell your student that in Sequoyah's time, the Cherokee inhabited the region that is now the states of Tennessee, North Carolina, South Carolina, Georgia, and Alabama. Near the end of Sequoyah's life, in the late 1830s, the U.S. government forcibly removed the Cherokee from their homelands to what is now the state of Oklahoma.

   For more information on Sequoyah and the Cherokee Language, you may wish to visit www.sequoyahmuseum.org.

2. Read

Have your student read "Sequoyah's Great Invention" in *American Lives and Legends*, pages 32-34.

3. Questions

Have your student write the answers to the questions in his Reading Notebook. If he has difficulty, have him read the relevant part of the story aloud.

1. What were the "talking leaves" Sequoyah admired?
   The "talking leaves" were the letters that the settlers and soldiers wrote to each other and to their families back home.

2. Why did Sequoyah want the Cherokee to learn to put words on "talking leaves"?
   Sequoyah wanted the Cherokee to learn to put words on "talking leaves" so they could have a way to write down their words and thoughts.

3. Describe the system of writing that Sequoyah created.
   Accept any reasonable response, for example: Sequoyah created a system in which symbols represented the different sounds in the Cherokee language.

4. Summarize the test the Cherokee Nation leaders gave Sequoyah and his daughter, Ayoka.
   Accept any reasonable response, for example: The leaders made Ayoka leave the room. They each told Sequoyah a story. Sequoyah wrote the stories down. Then Ayoka came back into the room and read aloud the stories Sequoyah had written.

4. Discuss

Discuss today's reading. If you wish, have your student write a paragraph in response to one of the questions.

1. What were the Cherokee able to do after Sequoyah invented the written language? Why is that important?
2. Inventing the written language was not easy. It took Sequoyah a long time, and he did not know if he would succeed. Why do you think he never gave up?

5. Activities

Ordinary People, Extraordinary Lives

Have your student complete an Ordinary People, Extraordinary Lives page for Sequoyah. As necessary, guide your student to write his name and the area where he lived on the lines. Your student should then write a paragraph that tells about Sequoyah's extraordinary accomplishment, and, if he wishes, draw a picture. Remind your student to give at least one reason why the accomplishment was extraordinary in support of his opinion.

Putting It All Together

Have your student staple his five Ordinary People, Extraordinary Lives pages into a book. He may make a cover for it if he wishes. Review the people and their achievements with him. Then discuss the following questions to synthesize and draw conclusions from the information.

1. What do all five people have in common?

    Accept any reasonable answer, for example: They all did something important for the sake of others.

2. Why do you think others wrote biographies, stories, or poems about them?

3. Which story did you like the best? Why?

    Guide your student to communicate which kind of writing most appealed to him—the biographies, the stories, the autobiography, or the poetry. Encourage him to explain why he liked the writing and how it helped him to appreciate the person's accomplishments.

4. What do you most want to remember about these stories? Why?

After your discussion, you may wish to have him write a response to question 2, 3, or 4 on the inside cover of his book (if he chose to create one) or in his Reading Notebook.

Lesson 8: People to Remember

Compare and contrast the lives of historical figures, and creatively present one person's accomplishments.

Objectives

Demonstrate comprehension of text.
Describe a character using evidence from the text.
Compare and contrast information.

Student Page

People to Remember

Materials

Ordinary People, Extraordinary Lives booklet
Important Places in American History map
optional: poster board
optional: glue or tape
optional: index cards
optional: crayons, markers, or colored pencils
optional: hanger
optional: hole punch
optional: string

Think Ahead

Discuss the following with your student.

Review your Ordinary People, Extraordinary Lives pages. What was each person's extraordinary accomplishment?

By reviewing these pages, your student will be preparing for the following discussion and project.

2. An Extraordinary Life

Engage in a discussion and have your student do a prewriting activity to prepare for the project in the next part of the lesson.

Discuss three of the historical figures from the unit with your student. The goal of the discussion is to describe each person's motivations and character. Discuss:

1. Why was each person's accomplishment unusual or extraordinary?

2. Why did the person achieve his or her goals? How did his or her accomplishment affect others?
    Guide your student to see that these people were all very determined individuals who worked hard or had great obstacles to overcome.

3. How were their accomplishments alike? How were they different?

   You may wish to point out to your student that while their accomplishments varied, each person did something that no one else thought they would be able to do, or succeeded in spite of hardship or disadvantages. For example: Benjamin Franklin was a poor runaway with little formal education; Phillis Wheatley was a slave; Paul Revere was a citizen, not a soldier; Sybil Ludington was a teenager; and Sequoyah developed a previously non-existent writing system.

Have your student divide a sheet into three columns and write the name of one person you discussed at the top of each column. Underneath each name, he should list words and phrases that describe the person. He may use the same word for more than one character. For example, under all three, he might write, "determined." Discuss his lists and guide him to pick and write down two words or phrases that he thinks describe the most important qualities the characters share.

You might want to prompt your student with questions like the following:
- Which people are willing to risk their lives for the sake of others? Which people devoted their lives, or a large part of their lives, to a particular idea or cause?
- Do the people expect rewards for their accomplishments? Why do they receive rewards? Why do we remember them today?
- Did anyone have to ask them for help? Or did they take action on their own?

3. Preserving the Past

The purpose of this project is to build on the previous discussion and prewriting in order to understand why people's lives and accomplishments are preserved through history and to take an active part in the application of such knowledge.

Discuss the following questions with your student to generate ideas about why and how history is kept and shared.

1. What other ways do people have to remember the past and keep history alive for others?

   Examples include: People build museums and create exhibits. They make art, write music, create scrapbooks, or produce movies.

2. Why do you think it's important to do so?

Your student may complete one of the three projects or use the suggestions as a springboard for his own ideas. He may look back at the stories, his Important Places in American History and his Ordinary People, Extraordinary Lives pages for ideas and information. You may also wish to encourage him to do additional research. The goal of this project is not only to present information from one of the biographies, but also to develop the student's engagement in and enjoyment of history and literature.

For any project, when he finishes, go over his writing with him. If needed, prompt him to go back to the stories to find specific examples for his opinions. Then have him check his writing to correct any errors. Encourage him to share his project with others.

Make a Museum Exhibit

Have your student create a museum exhibit on a piece of poster board or a mobile. If he chooses the poster board, have him plan his exhibit before he begins. You may wish to have him write on index cards and then glue or tape the index cards to the poster. If he chooses the mobile, he may write on one side of each index card and draw on the other, draw or cut out pictures separate from the writing, or tie on representative objects.

Make sure your student provides specific details and examples from the biography to support the following:
- A picture or drawing of the person
- Four sentences that tell important facts about the person
- Four sentences describing the person's accomplishment
- Two sentences that explain how people were affected by their accomplishment
- Two adjectives that describe the person with examples that support your opinion

Create a Stamp

Have your student design a stamp for one of the people in the unit, and write a nomination for the person and the stamp design. Encourage your student to write the first paragraph of the nomination about why the person should be chosen for the stamp, and the second paragraph about why the design should be chosen for the person. He may draw his stamp design on the same paper on which he writes his nomination, or he may draw it separately.

Make sure your student provides specific details and examples from the biography to support the following:
- The person's name
- What the person did that was extraordinary
- Why it was extraordinary
- How it affected others
- Two adjectives that describe the person with examples that support your opinion
- The reason why your design should be chosen, and how your design is representative of the person's life or his or her extraordinary accomplishment

Tell All About It

Have your student give an oral report or presentation about one person from the unit. He may write and read aloud a report, or he may write and give a speech as if he were the person. If he chooses to write a report, he may enjoy creating a poster or bringing objects to accompany his presentation. If he chooses to give a speech and act out the character, he may enjoy dressing up as the character and bringing props to accompany his speech.

Make sure your student provides specific details and examples from the biography to support the following:
- The person's name, date, and place where he or she lived
- What was happening in the United States at the time
- The person's extraordinary accomplishment
- Why the person is important
- Two adjectives that describe the person with examples that support your opinion
- How the person's accomplishment affected others

As necessary, remind your student that a character giving a speech would use *I, me*, and *mine* when referring to him or herself; for example, "My name in Benjamin Franklin. I am the tenth son in my family."

Lesson 9: Unit Assessment: Early American Lives

Check your student's recall and understanding with the Unit Assessment. When your student has finished the assessment, enter the results online.

Objectives
Demonstrate comprehension of text.
Identify main events of the plot.
Compare and contrast information.

Lesson Notes
Make sure your student understands the directions for the Unit Assessment, and then have him complete the assessment on his own. (He should not refer to the *American Lives and Legends* book while doing the assessment.)

Part 1: Who Said It?

Answers:
1. d
2. b
3. a
4. c
5. e

Part 2: Two Extraordinary Lives

Your student should write an essay of four paragraphs in which he identifies and describes two historical figures, their accomplishments, and how their accomplishments affected others. He should support his opinions with facts from the text.

Look back to your student's Ordinary People, Extraordinary Lives pages and People to Remember project for examples of the kind of qualities and evidence he should write about.

Unit 8: Stories of Washington Irving

Read "Rip Van Winkle," an American legend. Describe and understand the importance of the setting and the figurative language used to describe the setting. Understand Rip Van Winkle's character traits, and predict how his character traits foreshadow the story's events. Understand Washington Irving's background.

Lesson 1: "Rip Van Winkle": Session 1

Discuss what a legend is. Describe the setting of "Rip Van Winkle" and its importance. Recognize figurative language and its effectiveness in describing the setting. Meet Rip Van Winkle. Choose an adjective to describe his character. Recognize how an understanding of these character traits contributes to foreshadowing.

Lesson Notes

In this unit, your student will be reading abridgements of two classic legends by the American author Washington Irving, "Rip Van Winkle" and "The Legend of Sleepy Hollow." For certain classic works of literature, there is a long tradition of presenting children with abridged works when the original prose is too complex for almost any young child to read. These abridgements retain the characters and life-lessons that can move and inspire young children, but present them in a form that is inviting to younger audiences. The goal of these abridgements is not to dilute the original work but to offer younger readers an early entry into the world of classical literature.

This is the first of three sessions on "Rip Van Winkle."

Objectives

Demonstrate comprehension of text.
Identify and interpret examples of figurative language.
Identify examples of foreshadowing.
Describe a character using evidence from the text.
Predict upcoming events.

Student Pages

"Rip Van Winkle": Session 1
Figures of Speech

Materials

American Lives and Legends, pages 36-43
map of the Hudson Valley and Catskill Mountains (optional)
colored pencils (optional)

Keywords

legend: a fictional story of a particular culture that has been handed down from generation to generation, and usually includes information about the past

figurative language: poetic language and figures of speech such as metaphor, simile, and personification

foreshadowing: a literary technique of using clues that suggest what is going to happen

1. Get Ready

Vocabulary

Go over the vocabulary words with your student before she reads the story.

clamber: (v.) to climb with great effort
The little boy *clambered* up his father's back and asked for a piggy-back ride.

gable: (n.) the triangular meeting point of a wall and the sloping ends of the roof
Just below the roof of the house, right underneath the *gable*, there was a small window which we assumed was inside the attic.

hues: (n.) shades of color
In the autumn, the leaves turn beautiful *hues* of red and gold.

incessantly: (adv.) without stopping or being interrupted
In the background, the children chattered *incessantly*, so I strained to hear my telephone conversation.

jerkin: (n.) a snug jacket that comes to the top of the hips
For his costume, the boy wore his regular pants, a shirt with a ruffled front, and a *jerkin* on top of his shirt.

latticed: (adj.) covered with wood in a criss-cross design
The criss-cross designs on the *latticed* windows reminded me of a gingerbread house.

peals: (n.) loud, echoing sounds
The joke was so funny that we burst into *peals* of laughter and just couldn't stop giggling.

quaff: (v.) to drink deeply
I *quaffed* my lemonade quickly because I was very thirsty.

rubicund: (adj.) with a reddish skin tone
After being out in the sun and fresh air all day, her cheeks had a *rubicund* glow.

termagant: (adj.) quarrelsome, abusive, or shrewish
My *termagant* neighbor creates difficulties over the smallest issues; he even yells at my children if they bounce their ball too loudly.

vehemently: (adv.) forcefully
She *vehemently* disagreed with his opinion, and the angry look on her face clearly demonstrated her feelings.

ninepins (n.) a form of bowling that was popular in the colonies
Just as some people today enjoy the modern game of bowling, some colonists enjoyed playing *ninepins.*

weathercock: (n.) a figure that turns in the wind to show wind direction
Check the *weathercock* to determine which way the wind is blowing.

Think Ahead

Discuss the following with your student.

1. "Rip Van Winkle" is a legend written by American author, Washington Irving. A *legend* is a story that is handed down from the past. It is often based on actions of a hero. Legends often contain historical facts, but sometimes the facts change over time and the legend becomes fiction. Legends may be

based on real historical characters. However, the facts about these real characters may not be true. For example, the story of George Washington chopping down the cherry tree is a legend. What are some other legends you have read?

2. "Rip Van Winkle" is set in the Catskill Mountains in the New York colony. The legend begins before the Revolutionary War. As necessary, remind your student that *setting* is where and when a story takes place. The setting for this story is the Catskill Mountains during colonial times. The colonies are still under British rule. You may wish to point out New York state, the Hudson Valley, and the Catskill Mountains on a map.

As needed, share the following background information on the story, region, and author with your student.

*   English explorer Henry Hudson first sailed into New York Bay in 1609. He sailed up the river that was eventually named for him—the Hudson River.
*   The Dutch settled this area in 1623 and called the region New Netherland.
*   New York City (which was called New Amsterdam) and the New Netherland colony were settled by primarily Dutch people.
*   George III was the king of England from 1760 to 1820. This story takes place during a time when colonists were settling America.
*   Washington Irving was born in New York City and lived from 1783 to 1859. When Irving lived in New York, many of its residents were Dutch. Irving heard stories from the Dutch, and he drew on these stories for a number of his published works. As a boy, Irving often wandered about the countryside he so often describes in his writing. Guide your student to notice Irving's descriptions of the setting as she reads.

2. Read

Have your student read Parts 1 and 2 of "Rip Van Winkle" in *American Lives and Legends*, pages 36-43.

3. Questions

Have your student write the answers to the questions in her Reading Notebook. If she has difficulty, have her read the relevant part of the story aloud.

1. Describe the setting of this legend.
    This legend is set in the Catskill Mountains in the Hudson Valley in New York. The mountains are very beautiful and the village is quaint.

2. How does Rip Van Winkle get along with the people in town?
    Rip gets along well with the children and many of the adults.

3. Describe the relationship between Rip and his wife.
    Rip and his wife do not get along. She yells at him frequently and thinks that he is lazy. He ignores her or shrugs his shoulders, which makes her angrier.

4. Describe the stranger Rip meets in the mountains.
    The stranger is a small man in old-fashioned Dutch clothing.

5. Where does the stranger lead Rip? Whom does he see?
    The stranger leads Rip to a group of peculiar men who are playing ninepins.

6. How does Rip feel among the group of men? What does he do?
    At first Rip is very frightened. Then he begins to relax and drinks with them.

7. Why is Rip concerned when he awakens from his sleep?
    He is afraid his wife will be angry with him for staying out all night.

4. Discuss

Discuss today's reading. If you wish, have your student write a paragraph in response to one of the questions.

1. Why do you think the stranger approaches Rip Van Winkle?

2. *Foreshadowing* is a literary technique of using clues that suggest what is going to happen. Writers use foreshadowing to create suspense, alert their readers to important ideas, or build their readers' expectations. Reread Irving's description of the men whom Rip meets in the mountain. Does the author's language give you any clues about these men? How does Rip Van Winkle feel about them? What do you think Irving is foreshadowing?
    Tip: Guide your student to see that Irving's description of the men foreshadows that something strange is going to happen. The men are peculiar, and "the whole group reminded Rip of something out of an old painting that he had seen in the village" (p. 41). The strangeness of the men makes Rip uneasy. He notices that "their faces were grave, and they kept a mysterious silence" (p. 41). Help your student to see that Irving foreshadows that something strange is going to happen by giving the reader these clues.

3. What differences does Rip notice when he awakens from his sleep? What do you think might happen next?

5. Activities

Figures of Speech
In this activity, your student will work with figurative language and learn to interpret it by paraphrasing what it means. Have your student complete the Figures of Speech page. She should interpret the examples of figurative language from the story and then try creating her own figurative language. To emphasize the difference between literal and figurative meanings, she may illustrate the literal meaning of one or more of the examples, if she wishes.

Tip: Help your student to understand that the use of figurative language rather than literal language helps to create a certain mood or feeling in the story and helps create sympathy for Rip Van Winkle. For example, ask her to explain the difference between these two sentences:

- Rip Van Winkle was happy to do nothing and waste his life.
- If left to himself, he would have been happy to whistle his life away.

Help your student to see that the first sentence gives the reader a negative impression of Rip Van Winkle, whereas the figurative language ("happy to whistle his life away") used in the second sentence, which Washington Irving wrote, helps to create sympathy and makes Rip Van Winkle likable, in spite of his faults.

Answers will vary. Your student's responses should convey ideas similar to the following:
1. On a clear day the mountains look blue or purple.
2. They would rather go hungry than have to work to eat.
3. He'd be happy to do nothing with his life as long as it is pleasant.
4. Nasty people get nastier or hurtful remarks become meaner as they become more frequent.
5. He did the same thing at the same time every day.
6. His eyes rolled around; he couldn't see clearly.

Accept any reasonable answer for your student's own use of figurative language. Examples are:
*   A starry night – glittering diamonds in the sky
*   The sun reflecting on the water – light dancing on the water
*   A person who walks with very straight posture – walking like a ruler
*   A field that is covered with snow – cold blanket of the softest cotton

Character Foreshadowing

In this activity, your student will examine descriptions of Rip Van Winkle's character to determine whether the author foreshadows what happens to Rip. Ask your student to reread the paragraphs on page 37 describing Rip Van Winkle. Then have her choose an adjective that describes Rip Van Winkle and identify specific examples from the text that support the example. Next, have your student explain why the author likely gave such great detail to describe Rip's character. Finally, have your student predict what may happen in the story. What does Rip's laziness foreshadow?

Talk about reasons why authors use foreshadowing, such as suspense, curiosity, and engagement.

Discuss the items below in detail. Your student should answer them in her Reading Notebook.

*   After you read these paragraphs, choose an adjective to describe Rip Van Winkle. (Your student will likely offer the adjective *lazy;* however, another adjective is acceptable if it is supported by the text.)

*   List specific examples to support the adjective you have chosen. (Examples might include: Rip would just as soon "whistle away the day"; Rip did not like to work; Rip couldn't do his family duty and keep his farm in order.)

*   The author could have just chosen an adjective or two to describe the character. Why did the author go into such great detail about the character's actions? (The detail makes the story more interesting; it paints a "word picture" for the reader. Specific details can tell much more about a character than a simple adjective can.)

After your discussion, have your student predict what might happen in the story.

Lesson 2: "Rip Van Winkle": Session 2

Compare and contrast Rip's experiences before he goes up to the mountain and after he returns to his village. Consider Rip's perspective on these events.

Lesson Notes
This is the second of three sessions on "Rip Van Winkle."

Objectives
Demonstrate comprehension of text.
Compare and contrast characters.
Compare and contrast settings.
Predict upcoming events.

Student Pages
"Rip Van Winkle": Session 2
Rip Van Winkle: Before and After

Materials
American Lives and Legends, pages 43-47
paper
colored pencils

1. Get Ready

Vocabulary
Go over the vocabulary words with your student before she reads the story.

addled: (v.) confused
I am feeling dizzy and rather *addled*; I think I should sit down.

cur: (n.) a mutt
That dog isn't a purebred; he's a *cur*.

piping: (adj.) high-pitched and loud
The little girl threw a tantrum in the storm and everyone could hear her *piping* voice and her screaming.

riot: (n.) an outburst of disorder by a group of people
The police were afraid that there might be a *riot* because people were so upset; however, everyone remained calm and orderly.

Tory: (n): an American who upheld the cause of the British Crown, instead of colonial independence
During the Revolutionary War era, colonists who did not want independence from Britain identified themselves as *Tories*.

scepter: (n.) a royal staff, or baton, that shows authority
The king sat on his throne wearing his crown and holding his *scepter*.

tavern: (n.) an inn
We stopped at the *tavern* for food, drink, and rest.

Think Ahead

Discuss the following with your student.

1. Summarize Parts 1 and 2 of "Rip Van Winkle." In your summary, tell:
    *   Where the story takes place
    *   How Rip gets along with others in the village
    *   Where Rip goes when he leaves the village
    *   What happens to Rip on the mountain

2. Describe how Rip feels when he wakes up. What changes does he notice? What do you think he will find when he reaches the village?

2. Read

Have your student read Part 3 of "Rip Van Winkle" in *American Lives and Legends*, pages 43-47.

3. Questions

Have your student write the answers to the questions in her Reading Notebook. If she has difficulty, have her read the relevant part of the story aloud.

1. What surprises Rip when he nears the village?
    He sees people he doesn't recognize, and they don't recognize him.

2. How have the people in the village changed?
    The people dress and act differently.

3. How do the people and dogs react to Rip as he enters the village?
    The people make fun of him and the dogs snarl at him.

4. Give at least three examples of how the village has changed.
    The village is larger. It is filled with people. Rip doesn't recognize the names of the people. Rip's house has fallen to ruin. The inn is gone; it has been replaced by the Union Hotel. There is now an American flag flying.

5. Why does the man in the cocked hat accuse Rip of being a Tory? What does this accusation mean?
    The man accuses Rip of being a Tory because Rip says he is a loyal subject of the king.

6. Who might the person leaning against the tree be? Support your answer with details from the story.
    Accept any reasonable answer, as long as it is supported by story details. Your student is likely to say that this person is Rip's son—because he has the same name and the two look so much alike.

4. Discuss

Discuss today's reading. If you wish, have your student write a paragraph in response to one of the questions.

1. How does the landscape tell Rip that he is in the same place?
2. Why is the man with the cocked hat angry at Rip for being a loyal subject of the king?
3. What other changes in the village show that there has been a change in the political situation?
    > Tip: Guide your student to notice the Union Hotel, the American flag, and the statue of General
    > Washington. Remind her that American history (i.e., the Revolutionary War) is reflected in the
    > village. Invite your student to turn to page 45. Explain that the Revolutionary War is the reason for
    > the flag: "the stars and stripes." Also discuss the reference to "heroes of seventy-six" and explain
    > that it is a reference to the year 1776 and American independence.
4. Based on story events to this point, what do you think happened to Rip?

5. Activities

Comparing and Contrasting

In this activity, discuss comparing and contrasting with your student. Encourage her to recognize that authors may make direct comparisons and contrasts by using words such as *like* and *unlike.* Many times, however, authors leave it to the reader to compare and contrast. Invite your student to recall examples or create examples of direct comparisons and contrasts in this story, as well as those in which the author leaves it to the reader to create comparisons and contrasts. Have her complete the Rip Van Winkle: Before and After page using the questions below. Then discuss her work.

*   List at least three ways in which Rip has changed. (Sample answers: Many of his features look older. He has grown a long, gray beard. He is sore. He feels confused. He feels sad.) Your student may wish to draw a picture of how she imagines Rip looked before he went up to the mountain and how he looks now.

*   List at least three ways in which Rip is treated differently in the town. (Sample answers: Rip is not recognized. Dogs are not kind to Rip. Children are not kind to Rip. The adults are not kind to Rip.)

Rip's Journal

Your student will continue her exploration of Rip Van Winkle's character by creating a journal entry from Rip's *perspective*. Remind your student that *perspective* is the way a person sees or feels about things. As necessary, help her to follow the instructions and write her entry in her Reading Notebook.

Imagine that you are Rip Van Winkle. How would you feel about what has happened to you? Using your answers to the questions above, imagine that you are Rip. Write a journal entry to explain how you feel. Be sure to explain why you feel the way you do. Complete this activity in your Reading Notebook.

A Family Journal (optional)

How might Rip's son and daughter feel upon the return of their father? In this activity, your student will take a *different perspective* on the story's events. She will imagine she is the son or daughter and write a journal entry describing the day of Rip's return and how she felt.

Lesson 3: "Rip Van Winkle": Session 3

Identify Rip's role as a storyteller and town historian.

Lesson Notes
This is the third and final session of "Rip Van Winkle."

Objectives
Demonstrate comprehension of text.
Identify the role of characterization in plot.
Identify the elements of a legend.

Student Pages
"Rip Van Winkle": Session 3

Materials
American Lives and Legends, pages 47-51
paper
colored pencils or markers

1. Get Ready

Vocabulary
Go over the vocabulary words with your student before she reads the story.

> **inhabitants:** (n.) people who live in a specific place
> The *inhabitants* of the town were extremely welcoming to our tour group.

> **totter:** (v.) to move unsteadily
> When my baby sister was first learning to walk, my parents took a lot of video of her *tottering* around our house.

> **yoke of England:** (n.) a figure of speech referring to British rule
> The colonists' desire to be free of the *yoke of England* led to the American Revolution.

Tip: Explain to your student that a yoke is a restraint for oxen. Help her to see that expression "yoke of England" doesn't just refer to British rule, but it implies an unwelcome restraint.

Think Ahead
Discuss the following with your student.

1. Summarize yesterday's reading. In your summary, tell:
   - How Rip has changed since the beginning of the story
   - How people and animals treat him differently when he returns
   - How the town has changed while Rip was sleeping
   - How Rip feels when he returns
2. At the end of Part 3, Rip says, "I can't tell what's my name . . . " Why does he say this?
3. What kind of a life do you think that Rip will have in the village? What can he do that will be helpful and useful to the people?

---

2. Read

Have your student read "Rip Van Winkle" in *American Lives and Legends*, pages 47-51.

3. Questions

Have your student write the answers to the questions in her Reading Notebook. If she has difficulty, have her read the relevant part of the story aloud.

1. Who is the man leaning against the tree, the one who looks just like Rip Van Winkle did when he was young?
      This is Rip Van Winkle's son.

2. Who is the woman who walks up to Rip Van Winkle with the baby in her arms?
      She is Rip's daughter.

3. How is Peter Vanderdonk helpful to Rip?
      He recognizes Rip and says that Rip is the person he claims to be.

4. The author uses figurative language when he describes how people in the village reacted to Rip's story: "The neighbors stared when they heard it. Some winked at each other, and put their tongues in their cheeks." (p. 48) What does this mean and why do the people react this way?
      This is figurative language that means Rip's story was not believed by everyone.

5. Why does Rip prefer making friends among the younger people?
      Accept any reasonable answer, as long as it is supported by story details. Sample answer: Rip liked to tell stories, and the children liked to listen.

6. How does Rip live out his days?
      Rip becomes a storyteller in the village.

7. At the end of the story, the author explains that people say they hear Henry Hudson and his crew playing ninepins during a thunderstorm. What does the author mean?
      Earlier in the story (p. 49), the author wrote that Henry Hudson came back with his ghostly crew to play ninepins. He explained that Hudson was watching "over the river and the great city called by his name." Thunder can sound like bowling.

4. Discuss

Discuss today's reading. If you wish, have your student write a paragraph in response to one of the questions.

1. How does "Rip Van Winkle" fit the description of a legend?
      Tip: Remind your student that this story combines historical facts (the Revolutionary War) and historical people (Henry Hudson) with fiction.

2. How can a legend help history come to life?

3. Why do you think the author writes that Rip varied his story each time he told it?
    Tip: Guide you student to see that this is a reference to the nature of legends. They vary each
    time they are told.

4. Did your predictions about this legend come to pass? Support your answer with story details.

5. Activity

Becoming a Historian
In this activity, your student will consider the importance of transmitting personal historical accounts and
investigate the relationship between these transmissions and legends. Discuss the importance of people
passing along their personal accounts of history. If appropriate, you may wish to encourage your student
to recall examples from her own family's personal history. What stories has she learned from her elders?
What stories has she told others about her own experiences?

Explain that Rip transmits both a personal history, and a history of the town, in the story "Rip Van Winkle."
By explaining how certain historical events affected him and by discussing his own experiences, Rip
creates a personal history. Tell your student that people can breathe life into history by explaining
historical events and how those events affected them.

Discuss the questions below in detail.

*   Explain how Rip becomes a historian. (He tells the story of life before the revolution.)
*   Why is Rip more valuable as a historian than most of the other people in the village? (Rip lived
    through a time when most of the villagers hadn't yet been born—or a time when they were too young
    to remember historical details.)

After your discussion, have your student create an illustrated book of the village's history from Rip's point
of view. Guide her to choose events that occurred before Rip's lifetime (e.g., the founding of the village by
the Dutch, or Hendrick Hudson's voyage with his crew), events that occurred during Rip's youth and
adulthood (e.g., being British subjects), events that occurred while Rip slept (e.g., the Revolutionary War),
and a description of life in the village upon Rip's awakening (e.g., being Americans). Tell your student to
include illustrations with brief captions.

When she is finished, she should bind her book together.

If you wish, also encourage your student to create a book with a personal historical account. Explain that
the book should include at least four important historical events. Stress the importance of historical
accuracy in reporting the events.

Lesson 4: "The Legend of Sleepy Hollow": Session 1

In Parts 1 and 2, the reader is introduced to Sleepy Hollow and the legend of the Headless Horseman, as well as Ichabod Crane. The reader learns how much Crane enjoys hearing about the legend, but how much it scares him.

Lesson Notes
This is the first of three sessions on "The Legend of Sleepy Hollow."

Objectives
Demonstrate comprehension of text.
Identify setting.
Describe a character using evidence from the text.
Make inferences and draw conclusions based upon textual evidence.

Student Page
"The Legend of Sleepy Hollow": Session 1

Materials
American Lives and Legends, pages 52-55
map of the Hudson Valley and Catskill Mountains (optional)

Keyword
figurative language: poetic language and figures of speech such as metaphor, simile, and personification

1. Get Ready

Vocabulary
Go over the vocabulary words with your student before she reads the story.

anaconda: (n.) a type of snake
Of all of the snakes in the jungle, I am most afraid of the *anaconda.*

apparition: (n.) a ghost-like figure
When I peered through the dusty basement window, I saw an *apparition* and was terrified, but it was only a dusty sheet.

drowsy: (adj.) sleepy
The *drowsy* toddler was rubbing her eyes and really needed to nap.

gazette: (n.) newspaper
The town's local newspaper is called the Village *Gazette.*

glen: (n.) a small valley
This quiet *glen* is the perfect place for our picnic; it has grassy banks and shady trees.

Hessian: (n.) a German soldier in the British forces during the American Revolution
German soldiers who fought in the British forces during the American Revolutionary War were called *Hessians.*

quavers: (n.) trembles in the voice
The candidate's speech was very strong and she delivered it well; there were no *quavers* in her voice when she spoke in front of the large audience.

shillings: (n.) British coins
When I was in London, I changed my money for British currency, and I had *shillings* jingling in my pockets.

Think Ahead
Discuss the following with your student.

1. Review the elements of a legend.

2. Find the Tappan Zee area of the Hudson River Valley on your map Remind your student that Irving wrote stories that he had heard from the Dutch.

2. Read

Have your student read Parts 1 and 2 of "The Legend of Sleepy Hollow" in *American Lives and Legends*, pages 52-55.

3. Questions

Have your student write the answers to the questions in her Reading Notebook. If she has difficulty, have her read the relevant part of the story aloud.

1. What is the setting of this legend? How is it like the setting of "Rip Van Winkle"?
    This legend, like "Rip Van Winkle," is set in the Hudson Valley area of New York.

2. Describe Sleepy Hollow. Find details in the text to support your description.
    Accept any reasonable. Your student should recognize that Sleepy Hollow is a quaint and pretty place with a mysterious air to it.

3. Remember that *figurative language* is poetic language and figures of speech such as metaphor, simile, and personification. Just as he did in "Rip Van Winkle," author Washington Irving uses figurative language to describe the setting of this legend. List at least two examples of figurative language.
    Answers will vary. Two examples are:
    "The people walk around as though they are in a dream." (p. 52)
    "Sometimes the wind rushes through the Hollow like a midnight blast." (p. 53)

4. Who is the most famous character in Sleepy Hollow and what is the legend about him?
    The most famous character is the Headless Horseman. Some say he is the ghost of a Hessian soldier who is buried in the churchyard. The legend says that he is looking for his lost head.

5. Ichabod Crane is compared to a "traveling gazette." What does this mean?
    He takes all the local gossip, one sort of "news," from house to house.

6. What are three things Crane enjoys doing in his spare time?
    He enjoys reading scary stories, giving music lessons, and listening to gossip and frightening tales from the local housewives.

7. What price does Crane pay for listening to the frightening stories?
    He is terrified on his walk home.

4. Discuss

Discuss today's reading. If you wish, have your student write a paragraph in response to one of the questions.

1. The author says that the "hollow has a strange, dreamy effect on its residents and on visitors to its valley." What do you think this effect is, and why do you think it might be important?
    Guide your student to see that the effect is to make people believe things that are somewhat fantastic, or might be unbelievable in another place. This is important because this effect *foreshadows* strange happenings in Sleepy Hollow.

2. The author writes that Ichabod Crane's name suited him well. Why does he say this?
    Guide your student to recognize that the description of the character is similar to how one would describe a crane. If you wish, show your student a picture of a crane to help her see the similarities between the bird and the description of Ichabod Crane. An illustration is available at www.m-w.com/mw/art/crane.htm.

3. What kinds of stories do people in Sleepy Hollow tell? Do you think that these stories seem out of place in this quiet town? Why or why not?

5. Activities

Character Sketch
In this activity, have your student develop a character sketch of Ichabod Crane.

Remind your student that readers learn about characters by paying attention to what they say and do, and what others say about them. Readers can also make inferences about characters. To make an inference means to think about the evidence in the story and draw conclusions based on that evidence.

Discuss with your student the following questions:

*   What does Ichabod Crane look like? (Ichabod Crane looks like a crane. He is lanky and awkward.)

*   Describe Ichabod Crane's relationship with his students. (He enjoys playing games with the boys if they have pretty sisters or mothers who are good cooks. He must be on good terms with his students because he lives in their homes and eats with them.)

*   How does Ichabod Crane interact with other people in the town? (He enjoys carrying gossip from house to house. He also likes listening to the women's stories of haunted happenings.)

*   Is Ichabod Crane a brave man or a fearful man? How do you know? (He is very frightened. The stories scare him.)

After your discussion, have your student draw conclusions about Ichabod Crane. In her Reading Notebook, she should write a paragraph describing the kind of person Ichabod Crane is. Then have her draw a picture of Ichabod Crane as she envisions him and write three important adjectives underneath the picture. Remind your student to use evidence from the story to support her ideas.

Lesson 5: "The Legend of Sleepy Hollow": Session 2

Investigate the characters of Katrina van Tassel and Brom Bones and describe their relationships with Ichabod Crane.

Lesson Notes

This is the second session on "The Legend of Sleepy Hollow."

Objectives

Demonstrate comprehension of text.

Describe a character using evidence from the text.

Make inferences and draw conclusions based upon textual evidence.

Student Page

"The Legend of Sleepy Hollow": Session 2

Materials

American Lives and Legends, pages 56-59

1. Get Ready

Vocabulary

Go over the vocabulary words with your student before she reads the story.

burly: (adj.) large and strong
The weightlifters were big, *burly* men with huge muscles.

feud: (n.) a serious quarrel that goes on for a long period of time
Romeo and Juliet is a famous love story of a couple that is kept apart by their parents' *feud*.

formidable: (adj.) having qualities that discourage other people from attacking
The dog certainly looked *formidable*, so it was a good thing that there was a fence with a sign that said, "Beware of Dog."

madcap: (adj.) crazy
My uncle is a real practical joker; he is always pulling a *madcap* stunt or trick on someone in the family.

mettle: (n.) courage
The fighter pilots were full of bravery, courage, and *mettle*.

pewter: (adj.) a metal that looks like silver
Is that tea set made of silver or *pewter*?

ruddy: (adj.) of a healthy red color
The healthy lifestyle and time spent outdoors must agree with Joan because her cheeks have turned a *ruddy* color.

smitten: (adj.) taken with or captured by
The new mother is so *smitten* with love for her new baby that she can't focus on anything else.

steed: (n.) horse
If you are going to journey on horseback, you will want to make certain that your *steed* is strong and trustworthy.

Think Ahead
Discuss the following with your student.

1. Summarize Parts 1 and 2 of "The Legend of Sleepy Hollow." In your summary, tell:
   • Where the story takes place
   • What Ichabod Crane is like
   • What frightens Ichabod Crane

2. Describe how Ichabod Crane feels when he walks home.

2. Read

Have your student read Part 3 of "The Legend of Sleepy Hollow" in *American Lives and Legends*, pages 56-59.

3. Questions

Have your student write the answers to the questions in her Reading Notebook. If she has difficulty, have her read the relevant part of the story aloud.

1. Describe Katrina Van Tassel.
   Sample answer: She is lovely and wealthy. Many men compete for her affection.

2. Why does Ichabod like Katrina? How does he imagine his life with her?
   He likes her because she is lovely and because her father is rich. He would like to use her father's money to go west with Katrina and have many children.

3. Who is Ichabod's chief rival for Katrina?
   Abraham Van Brunt or Brom Bones.

4. Why do the people in town give Abraham Van Brunt the nickname Brom Bones?
   Brom is the Dutch nickname for Abraham. They call him Brom Bones because he is so strong.

5. What are the names of Brom's and Ichabod's horses?
   Ichabod's horse is named Gunpowder. Brom's horse is named Daredevil.

6. How does Brom treat Ichabod?
   Brom treats Ichabod poorly because the two men are in a feud. He plays pranks on Ichabod and wants to fight him.

7. What happens during the party at the Van Tassels home?
   Ichabod dances with Katrina and enjoys the party. Brom sulks in a corner.

4. Discuss

Discuss today's reading. If you wish, have your student write a paragraph in response to one of the questions.

1. Summarize the relationships between the main characters: Crane, Bones, and Katrina van Tassel.
   Sample answer: Crane and Bones both want the attention of Katrina van Tassel. They feud over her. We don't yet know which one, if either, Katrina likes.

2. Do you think the author has foreshadowed later events through these relationships? Why or why not?
   Accept any reasonable answer, as long as it is supported. Sample answer: Yes. Crane and Bones are feuding over Katrina van Tassel. This could lead to a fight between the two.

5. Activity

Character Sketch
In her Reading Notebook, have your student complete a second character sketch to investigate the character of Brom Bones.

As necessary, remind your student that readers learn about characters by paying attention to what they say and do, and what others say about them.

Discuss the following questions with your student:
- What does Brom Bones look like?
- What is Brom Bones famous for?
- How do people in the town react to Brom Bones?
- Why does Brom Bones play pranks?
- Why doesn't Brom Bones fight Ichabod Crane for Katrina's love?
- Is Brom Bones a brave man or a fearful man? How do you know?

After your discussion, have your student draw conclusions about Brom Bones. In her Reading Notebook, she should write a paragraph describing the kind of person Brom Bones is. Then have her draw a picture of Brom as she envisions him and write three important adjectives underneath the picture. Remind your student to use evidence from the story to support her ideas. Have your student save this sketch for a future lesson.

Lesson 6: "The Legend of Sleepy Hollow": Session 3

Ichabod Crane confronts his greatest fear—the Headless Horseman. His actions and behavior add to the mystery of "The Legend of Sleepy Hollow." Compare and contrast the characters of Ichabod Crane and Brom Bones.

Lesson Notes
This is the final session of "The Legend of Sleepy Hollow."

Objectives
Demonstrate comprehension of text.
Describe a character using evidence from the text.
Compare and contrast characters.

Student Pages
"Legend of Sleepy Hollow": Session 3
Compare and Contrast Characters

Materials
American Lives and Legends, pages 60-64

1. Get Ready

Vocabulary
Go over the vocabulary words with your student before she reads the story.

ado: (n.) trouble
William Shakespeare wrote a play entitled *Much Ado About Nothing,* which means a lot of trouble over nothing.

crestfallen: (adj.) sad and disappointed
The little boy was *crestfallen* when he didn't win the contest.

dismal: (adj.) gloomy
The clouds were gray, the sky was stormy, and the whole day was *dismal* and gloomy.

jilted: (v.) harshly broke up with someone
Doris *jilted* Sam and she is now dating Robert.

melancholy: (adj.) very sad
The song was so *melancholy* that the choir's singing brought tears to every member of the audience's eyes.

parched: (adj.) extremely dry
The *parched* ground gratefully absorbed the rainfall after the long drought.

pommel: (n.) a knob-shaped piece the rider holds onto at the front of a saddle
Sarah sat astride the horse and held onto the *pommel* on the saddle in order to learn to ride.

supernatural: (adj.) beyond known forces of nature
We sat by the campfire and told scary stories of *supernatural* events.

Think Ahead

Discuss the following with your student.

1. Summarize the reading from Parts 1-3 of "The Legend of Sleepy Hollow." Make sure your student includes the following:
   - Where the story takes place
   - What Ichabod Crane is like
   - What frightens Ichabod Crane
   - What Brom Bones is like
   - What Katrina van Tassel is like
   - What the relationships between Crane, Bones, and Katrina van Tassel are like
   - What happens at the party

2. At the end of Part 3, Bones is brooding by himself in a corner. Why?

2. Read

Have your student read "The Legend of Sleepy Hollow" in *American Lives and Legends*, pages 60-64.

3. Questions

Have your student write the answers to the questions in her Reading Notebook. If she has difficulty, have her read the relevant part of the story aloud.

1. What kinds of stories do people tell at the party?
   Some were telling stories from the Revolutionary War. Others were telling stories about the Headless Horseman.

2. Why is Ichabod Crane sad when he leaves the party?
   When your student reads this section, she can probably guess that Katrina has broken up with Crane. This information is mentioned later in the story.

3. What happens after Ichabod Crane leaves the party?
   He is followed by someone he believes to be the Headless Horseman.

4. Why does Ichabod Crane think he'll be safe after he crosses the bridge?
   Bones told a story about the Headless Horseman disappearing after Bones crossed the bridge.

5. What happens after Ichabod Crane crosses the bridge?
   The figure continues to chase him.

6. There are two opinions about why Ichabod Crane disappeared. What are they?
   One says that he was embarrassed by his fear and by losing Katrina. The other says that he was "spirited away by supernatural means."

7. Why do you think Brom Bones laughs at the mention of a pumpkin? Give at least one reason to support your answer.
   Bones probably played a prank on Crane and threw the pumpkin at him.

4. Discuss

Discuss today's reading. If you wish, have your student write a paragraph in response to one of the questions.

1. Do you believe that Brom Bones really does see the Headless Horseman one night and dares him to race? Why or why not? Support your answer with details from the text.
    Guide your student to see that this information supports the characterization of Brom as a braggart and a daredevil.

2. Explain how Ichabod Crane tries to escape the Headless Horseman.

3. What do you think happened to Ichabod Crane after he was hit in the head? Support your answer with details about Ichabod from the story.

4. Why do you think that Washington Irving leaves the end of the story a little mysterious?
    Guide your student to see that the mystery helps to fuel the legend. No one is sure what really happens to Ichabod Crane but the story gets told over and over.

5. Activity

Compare and Contrast Characters

Have your student compare and contrast Ichabod Crane and Brom Bones. She should use her two character sketches to help her complete the chart on the Compare and Contrast Characters page. If needed help her find the following information in the story.

*   Three important adjectives that describe the character (Your student can take these from her two sketches.)
*   A description of what each character looks like (Ichabod is tall, gaunt, and awkward. Brom is burly and strong.)
*   A description of how the character gets along with other people in town (Ichabod gets along well with the women of the town and he plays with the children. People are a little in awe of Brom. They also admire him.)
*   A description of how each character feels about Katrina (Both men like Katrina very much.)
*   A description of how each character reacts to the Headless Horseman (Ichabdod is terrified; Brom allegedly challenges the Headless Horseman.)
*   A description of each character's strengths (Ichabod is a good teacher and a good singer. He also shares stories. Brom has physical strength and courage.)
*   A description of each character's weaknesses (Ichabod frightens easily. Brom plays pranks.)

When your student is finished, discuss the sharp contrasts between the two characters. Help her to see that Irving sets the characters up to be opposites. Brainstorm possible reasons for this.

Lesson 7: Unit Assessment: Stories of Washington Irving

Check your student's recall and understanding with the Unit Assessment.

Objectives
Demonstrate comprehension of text.
Describe a character using evidence from the text.

Lesson Notes
Make sure your student understands the directions for the Unit Assessment, and then have her complete the assessment on her own. (She should not refer to the *American Lives and Legends* book while doing the assessment.)

Part 1: Facts About the Story

Answers:
1. b
2. a
3. d
4. c
5. d

Part 2: Describe a Character

Your student should write four paragraphs that identify and describe either Rip Van Winkle, Ichabod Crane, or Brom Bones and give a reason why this character is a good character to include in a legend. She should support each adjective she chooses with an example from the text.

Look back to your student's Reading Notebook entries, her Rip Van Winkle Before and After page, her Character Sketches, and to her Compare and Contrast Characters page for examples of the descriptions and evidence she should write about.

Unit 9: Passing Moments

This unit presents poems that capture passing moments, such as a glimpse of a river from a bridge, a skateboard ride, or an apology for eating some plums. While some of these moments might seem slight or trivial, in the eyes and hands of the poet, each is invested with meaning and interest.

Lesson 1: Incidents and Messages

Analyze and interpret poems that find meaning in passing moments.

Objective
Interpret poetry and support interpretations with evidence from the text.

Student Pages
Incidents and Messages
Everyday Poetry

Materials
Classics for Young Readers, Vol. 5A: "The White Horse" (page146), "Incident" (page 145), and "This Is Just to Say" (page146)

First Reading: "The White Horse"

1. Get Ready

Vocabulary
Go over the vocabulary word with your student before he reads the poem.

> **halter:** (n.) straps put on a horse's head and used to lead a horse
> After putting a *halter* on the pony, the girl led him out of the stable.

2. Read

Have your student read "The White Horse" once silently and a second time aloud.

3. Discuss

1. What happens in the poem?
     A young person approaches a white horse, preparing to put a halter on the horse. The horse silently looks at the youth.

2. What do you think it means that "they are in another world"?
     Accept any reasonable answer. The youth and horse, looking at each other in silence (notice the near repetition of "silent" and "silence"), are not literally somewhere else but are experiencing some special connection, a moment of understanding that cannot be put into words.

Tip: Discuss how the closing words—"they are in another world"—change the whole experience of the poem. Up to that point, the poem could be read as simple description of a fairly ordinary action. Note that in the poem the youth approaches the horse with the halter but is never described as actually putting it on. In the passing moment during which the horse looks silently at the youth, something happens, some silent understanding is achieved, that takes the youth and horse out of the realm of our ordinary experience.

Second Reading: "Incident"

4. Get Ready

Vocabulary
Go over the vocabulary words with your student before he reads the poem.

> **incident:** (n.) a brief event; an event that causes trouble
> When the policeman caught the boy lighting firecrackers, he said, "Young man, let's go see your parents and discuss this *incident*."

> **whit:** (n.) a very small amount
> My uncle Charley is so absent-minded that most people think he hasn't got a *whit* of sense.

Think Ahead
Recall with your student the old childhood rhyme, "Sticks and stones may break my bones, but names can never hurt me." Discuss whether that has been true in your student's experience, or whether some names can hurt as much as sticks and stones.

> Note: The poem "Incident" by Countee Cullen contains a racial slur used toward African Americans. You may wish to prepare your student for this by discussing that the use of such language is not meant to offend readers, but instead to provide a realistic representation of the time in which Cullen was writing and the feelings the speaker in the poem experiences as a result of this slur. You may wish to use this poem and the use of this slur as a springboard for a discussion about racism and prejudice.

5. Read

Have your student read "Incident" once silently and a second time aloud. (You may want to read the poem aloud first.)

6. Discuss

1. Who is the speaker of the poem? What is the "incident" the title refers to? Describe what happens.
    The speaker is probably an adult who is telling the story of an incident that happened to him when he was eight years old. He says "I was eight and very small," and he uses the past tense ("I saw," "I was," "I smiled"), and he says, "That's all that I remember."

Tip: Your student might first identify the speaker as the eight-year-old child. If so, help him see the evidence in the poem that suggests an older person looking back on a childhood experience.

2. In the first stanza, how does the speaker feel? Which words show you this?
    In the first stanza he is very happy: "heart-filled, head-filled with glee."

3. What is the "incident" the title refers to?
    While riding along in Baltimore, the speaker sees another child staring at him. The speaker smiles but the other child sticks out his tongue and calls the speaker a crude and hurtful name.

4. The poem says that after the incident the speaker stayed in Baltimore for several months, "from May until December." Why do you think this incident is all that the speaker remembers of Baltimore?
    Answers will vary. You might discuss how a very painful experience can leave a lasting negative impression that overwhelms all the positive feelings or memories.

5. Why does the other child act in such an ugly manner?
    Answers will vary. You might want to discuss the concept of prejudice with your student.

    Tip: The poet, Countee Cullen, was an African American writer who lived from 1903 to 1946. Since the incident in the poem is an experience of racial prejudice, you might want to discuss this topic with your student. Assuming that the poem describes an experience Cullen had as a child, then he would have been eight years old in the year 1911, a time when many African Americans experienced segregation and discrimination in much of American life, including education, employment, housing, and health care.

Third Reading: "This Is Just to Say"

7. Get Ready

Vocabulary
Go over the vocabulary word with your student before he reads the poem.

> **icebox:** (n.) refrigerator
> Always put the milk back in the *icebox* or it will spoil.

Think Ahead
What makes a poem a poem? Talk with your student about what he expects from a poem. Does he expect (usually) rhyming words, or figurative language such as simile and metaphor? Ask him to think about how the next poem does or does not meet his expectations of what a poem should be.

8. Read

Have your student read "This Is Just to Say" once silently and a second time aloud. (You may want to read the poem aloud first.)

9. Discuss

1. In your own words describe what is happening in this poem.

    The speaker is telling someone, perhaps in a written note, that he has eaten the plums that the other person was saving for breakfast.

2. To whom do you think the speaker is talking or writing in this poem? What words make you think this?

    Answers will vary. The speaker is addressing someone who was "probably saving" the plums for breakfast. This might be the speaker's wife or someone else in the family. It is someone whose feelings the speaker cares about, since he asks, "Forgive me."

3. Did the speaker enjoy eating the plums? What specific words let you know?

    Yes, he enjoyed them very much; he says "they were delicious / so sweet / and so cold."

4. Look at the title of the poem. How does the title connect with the poem itself? What does the "This" in the title refer to?

    The title serves in effect almost as the first line of the poem—when you read the poem aloud, the title is part of the sense and meaning of the first two stanzas. The word "This" in the title refers to the following words, that is, the poem itself. The poem, then, might be a note the speaker left for the person who was saving the plums for breakfast.

5. Can you imagine a situation in which someone might speak or write these words? Describe the situation.

    Answers will vary. For example: One night, after his wife had gone to bed, the speaker was hungry. He looked in the refrigerator and saw the plums. He ate them even though he knew that his wife was probably saving them for breakfast. So he wrote her this poem as a message to explain what he did, and to apologize.

6. On a sheet of paper, write the poem, including the title, as two or three sentences. How does it change the poem to write it this way?

    Answers will vary. For example, when the words are written as sentences, then they seem less like a poem. When the words are not arranged in lines and stanzas, then they seem more like just a brief note.

7. Do you think "This Is Just to Say" is a poem at all? What makes it a poem?

    Answers will vary. In part, "This Is Just to Say" is a poem because the poet has arranged the words in poetic form—in lines and stanzas—which makes us pay attention in a way that we might not pay attention to a note left on a scrap of paper on a countertop. It suggests that this apparently small incident—eating plums and leaving a note of apology—has some significance that might not be obvious at first glance.

Activity

10. Everyday Poetry

William Carlos Williams (1883-1963), who wrote "This Is Just to Say," was not only a poet but also a doctor who lived in New Jersey. In his poems, he often paid attention to common everyday objects and everyday speech.

The activity sheet offers your student a choice of three activities that allow him to play with everyday language as Williams did in some of his poems. When you take everyday language and break the words into stanzas and lines, you give it the form of a poem. And when you do this, you see and hear the words in a new way.

Encourage your student to play around with how he breaks the lines and stanzas. This is easy to do if your student types the poem on a word processor. Then he can easily move blocks of text and see the different effects made by different line breaks.

Have your student complete one of the activities on the Everyday Poetry sheet, or more if he is enjoying them.

Lesson 2: Child's Play

Riding a skateboard, skating, and stealing a base in baseball—in today's poems, see how the poets bring these actions to life through their language, including metaphors, similes, and vivid verbs.

Objectives
Interpret poetry and support interpretations with evidence from the text.
Identify action as conveyed through vivid verbs in poems.
Identify metaphor.
Identify simile.
Compare and contrast poems.

Keywords
setting: where and when a story takes place

simile: a figure of speech that compares two things, usually using the words *like* or *as,* for example, "like a thief in the night," "quiet as a mouse."

metaphor: a figure of speech that suggests or states a comparison between two unlike things, without using such words as *like* or *as*, for example: The cat's eyes were emeralds shining in the night.

Student Page
Child's Play

Materials
Classics for Young Readers, Vol. 5A: "The Sidewalk Racer" (page 147), "Song Form" (page 148), and "Base Stealer" (page 148)

First Reading: "The Sidewalk Racer (or On a Skateboard)"

1. Get Ready

Vocabulary
Go over the vocabulary word with your student before he reads the poem.

> **asphalt:** (n.) a mixture of tar, gravel, and other materials used for paving roads; (adj.) made from asphalt
> On hot summer days, the *asphalt* road is too hot to cross with bare feet.

Think Ahead
Ask your student to describe a physical activity that he especially enjoys, such as riding a bike or swimming. Can he put into words the sensation he feels when he is completely involved in this activity?

2. Read

Have your student read "The Sidewalk Racer" once silently and a second time aloud. (You may want to read the poem aloud first.)

3. Discuss

1. What is the speaker doing in the poem?

    The speaker is riding a skateboard.

2. The first half of the poem is full of action, beginning with the first word, *skimming.* Identify four action verbs in the first half of the poem.

    swerve, curve, sway, speed

3. The poet uses *metaphor* to describe the experience of riding a skateboard. Remember, a metaphor suggests or states a comparison between two unlike things without using the words "like" or "as." In the metaphor in the second line of the poem, what is being compared to "an asphalt sea"? How is riding a skateboard like "skimming an asphalt sea"?

    The "asphalt sea" is the pavement or sidewalk. Answers will vary regarding how riding a skateboard is like "skimming an asphalt sea"—for example, your student might suggest that going up and down over the hills and bumps of the sidewalk is like going up and down on waves in the sea.

4. The next two metaphors compare the skater to different things. (See lines 6-8.) Write the metaphors here:

    I'm the sailor and the sail

    I'm the driver and the wheel

    Why does the speaker say that she is both "the sailor *and* the sail," and both "the driver *and* the wheel"? What does this tell us about the experience of riding a skateboard?

    These metaphors suggest that the speaker and the skateboard have become one, that the mover and the thing that moves have merged—in other words, when you ride a skateboard, it's as though the skateboard becomes part of you.

5. In the final metaphor of the poem (lines 9-12), to what does the speaker compare herself?

    She compares herself to a "single engine human automobile."

6. There are rhymes in this poem, but not always at the ends of the lines, where you usually find rhyming words in poetry. Read the poem aloud again and identify three pairs of rhyming words.

    swerve-curve

    sound-ground

    wheel-[mo]bile

7. Look at the shape of the poem on the page. The lines do not start evenly along the left margin, and some of the lines break in unexpected places. Why do you think the poet wrote the lines in the way she did?

    Answers will vary. For example, the shape of the lines on the page might remind your student of the shape of a skateboard. Or the symmetry of the lines might suggest the balance needed to ride a skateboard.

Second Reading: "Song Form"

4. Get Ready

Vocabulary
Go over the vocabulary word with your student before he reads the poem.

> **distinctions:** (n.) differences
> There seemed to be no *distinctions* between the twins—they looked the same, talked the same, and even smiled the same!

Think Ahead
Talk with your student about quiet moments when you feel the joy of just being alive.

5. Read

Have your student read "Song Form" once silently and a second time aloud. (You may want to read the poem aloud first.) (Note: The last line of the poem might look odd, but it is printed correctly in the book, just as the poet wrote it.)

Tip: Your student may notice that two names are listed for the poet. LeRoi Jones is an African American writer, born in 1934, who changed his name to Imamu Amiri Baraka.

6. Discuss

1. There are two people in the poem. Who are they and what are they doing?
    The two people are the speaker and "some kid." They are skating.

2. What is the *setting* of the poem? What time of day is it, and where are these people? Point to specific words and phrases that describe the setting.
    The setting is "uptown" on a "quiet" city street. It is very early morning—"Sun's not even up."

3. What happens in this passing moment between the speaker and the kid? Why does it matter that they do not have "to smile too tough" or "be very pleasant even to each other"?
    Answers will vary. Very little happens (and that's part of the point of the poem)—the speaker and the kid are just enjoying themselves as they skate. They do not have to recognize each other or interact with each other as they might under different circumstances, for example, when they might try to confront each other with tough smiles, or when they might have to strain to be pleasant to each other.

4. What kind of pleasure does the speaker in this poem get from skating? In particular, what do you think he means by "merely to be"?
    The speaker seems to be absorbed in the joy of moving along the quiet streets. He does not have to worry about anyone or anything else. He can just lose himself in the quiet joy of just being alive—"merely to be" is enough in itself.

Tip: You and your student might want to discuss why the poet divides the second use of "merely" with a comma: "mere, ly to be." There's no right answer. Perhaps the poet just felt a moment of playful pleasure in the rhyme of "ly" and "be" and wanted to draw attention to it.

Tip: You might want to go back and discuss the second line with your student: "no matter the distinctions that can be made." On this quiet morning, when the speaker and the kid are each feeling the joy of skating along otherwise empty streets, all differences—the "distinctions"—fade away. They do not have to worry about their different backgrounds or anything else that might cause tension between them.

5.   Compare and contrast the experience of riding a skateboard in "The Sidewalk Racer" to skating in "Song Form." Which is more active?

   "The Sidewalk Racer" is more active; the whole emphasis of the poem is on energy, action, movement: "I swerve. I curve, I sway; I speed…." In contrast, there is very little action or movement in "Song Form." The poem emphasizes the "quiet" of the scene (note that "quiet" is repeated three times). The pleasure of skating does not come from the action or movement, but from the calm pleasure in just being alive, "merely to be."

Third Reading: "The Base Stealer"

7. Get Ready

Vocabulary
Go over the vocabulary words with your student before he reads the poem.

   poise: (v.) to balance; to hold in a steady position
   The ballerina stood *poised* on one toe.

   taut: (adj.) tight
   When the line went *taut*, we knew a fish was on the hook.

   scattering: (n.) a small amount of something
   The man threw a *scattering* of crumbs on the ground for the pigeons.

   teeter: (v.) to wobble; to move unsteadily
   As I crossed the narrow log over the stream, I *teetered* and shook, but I didn't fall in!

   skitter: (v.) to move in a fast, light way
   I like to watch the water bugs *skitter* across the lake.

   taunt: (v.) to tease; to mock; to provoke with insulting words
   Sir Galahad remained calm even though the cruel knight *taunted* him by shouting, "You have the strength of a flea and the courage of a mouse!"

   ecstatic: (adj.) extremely joyful; wildly delighted
   When Melinda learned she had been given the lead role in the play, she was more than happy—she was *ecstatic*.

Think Ahead
Help your student picture a baseball game in his mind to prepare for reading the next poem.

8. Read

Have your student read "The Base Stealer" once silently and a second time aloud. (You may want to read the poem aloud first.)

9. Discuss

1. In your own words describe what is happening in the poem. Where is the base stealer? What is he doing?

    In a baseball game, a base runner is preparing to steal the next base. The runner is moving off one base and toward the other. He is moving around, "bouncing tiptoe" and "running a scattering of steps sidewise," "teasing" and "taunting" the other team with his movements, and waiting for just the right moment to take off for the next base.

2. The poet describes this moment with *similes*. A simile compares two things using *like* or *as*. In the second line, the base stealer is "pulled . . . taut like a tightrope-walker" between the bases. Find two other similes in the poem and write them below:

    bouncing "like a dropped ball" or like "a kid skipping rope"
    hovering "like an ecstatic bird"

    Tip: Discuss with your student the effect of the similes. They create the feeling of tension and movement. The similes show action and movement—"bouncing tiptoe like a dropped ball or a kid skipping rope," or hovering "like an ecstatic bird" (the picture of a hummingbird might come to mind, with the wings in rapid motion even as the bird remains apparently still). But all this movement is up-and-down or back-and-forth; it is *not* the forward movement that the whole poem is straining to keep in check until the very last line, indeed, the last word.

3. Identify the six vivid verbs in lines 7 and 8, and write them here:

    teeters, skitters, tingles, teases, taunts, hovers

4. Reread the last two lines of the poem. What is happening at the very end (when the poet writes, "— now!")? Read aloud the last line with expression. How will you vary the way you say "delicate," which is repeated four times? How will you say "now"?

    "Now!" is the signal that the base runner is off and running to try to steal the next base.

    Tip: Discuss with your student how to read the last line with expression that conveys the tension and energy of the scene. He might, for example, read each "delicate" quietly, starting almost at a whisper, then getting just slightly louder on each one, and then ending with an explosive burst on "now!"

Optional Activity

10. Act It Out

If your child would like to, have him act out the movements in "The Base Stealer" as you read the poem aloud—balancing with arms out and fingers pointed, bouncing in place, teetering back and forth, delicately leaning or inching forward, then bursting into a full-speed run.

Lesson 3: Moments in Nature

Today your student will look at the language that poets use as they depict passing moments in the natural world.

Objectives
Interpret poetry and support interpretations with evidence from the text.
Identify and explain personification.
Identify metaphor.
Identify alliteration.
Identify rhyme scheme.

Keywords
alliteration: use of words with the same or similar beginning sounds, for example, "Peter Piper picked a peck of pickled peppers"

metaphor: a figure of speech that suggests or states a comparison between two unlike things, without using such words as *like* or *as*, for example: The cat's eyes were emeralds shining in the night.

personification: giving human qualities to a thing or abstraction, for example: The kettle sang on the hearth.

rhyme scheme: the pattern of rhymes made by the final words or sounds in the lines of a poem, typically designated by a different letter of the alphabet to represent each rhyme

Student Pages
Moments in Nature
Rhyme Schemes

Materials
Classics for Young Readers, Vol. 5A, "The Tide in the River" (page 150), "The River Is a Piece of Sky" (page 149), and "Snow Toward Evening" (page 150)

First Readings: "The Tide in the River" and "The River Is a Piece of Sky"

1. Get Ready

Vocabulary
Go over the vocabulary words with your student before he reads the poem.

cockleshell: (n.) the wavy, rounded shell of a small water creature
The children found *cockleshells* in the tide pools.

cobblestone: (n.) a stone used to pave streets in former times
The horse's hooves clattered on the *cobblestones* as it pulled the wagon through the streets of old London.

Think Ahead

Have your student try to picture a river in his imagination. If he is standing on a bridge and looking down at the water, what does he see?

2. Read

Have your student read "The Tide in the River" once silently and a second time aloud. Then have him read "The River Is a Piece of Sky" once silently and a second time aloud. (You may want to read the poems aloud first.)

3. Discuss

1. In the last three lines of "The Tide in the River," the poet imagines the tide in the river as almost human. Explain how she *personifies* the tide.

    The poet says that the tide "turned over in its sleep," an action that people, not tides, normally do. (The personification suggests a still, sleepy presence, not consciously active, but moving even in its rest.)

2. How would you describe the *mood* of this poem? What effect does the repetition in the first three lines have on the mood?

    Accept any reasonable answer. For example, the mood might strike some readers as calm, still, and thoughtful. The repetition might seem almost hypnotic, and have an effect like a lullaby, calming and soothing—an impression consistent with the idea of "sleep" later in the poem.

3. Describe the perspective in "The River Is a Piece of Sky." Where exactly does the poet want you to imagine you are standing?

    The imagined perspective is from "the top of a bridge," looking down at the water of the river below.

4. How can a river be "a piece of sky"? What is the poet describing?

    The river is "a piece of sky" when the sky above is reflected in the calm, unbroken surface of the water.

5. When you throw things in, why do you know that the river is a river and not "a piece of sky"?

    When the objects fall into the water, they cause splashes, and so break the still reflection of the sky in the water: "The river has splashes, / The sky hasn't any."

6. The title of the poem is a figure of speech. What kind of figure of speech is it? (Hint: Is it a simile or metaphor?)

    It is a metaphor. (It states a comparison between two things without using "like" or "as": river = piece of sky.)

Second Reading: "Snow Toward Evening"

4. Get Ready

Vocabulary
Go over the vocabulary word with your student before he reads the poem.

> **intensely:** (adv.) very; extremely
> The heat from the fireplace was *intensely* hot.

Think Ahead
The title of this poem is worth noting, as it serves in effect to explain the poem.

5. Read

Have your student read "Snow Toward Evening" once silently and a second time aloud. (You may want to read the poem aloud first.)

6. Discuss

1. In this poem there is an "invisible blossoming tree" from which "millions of petals" are falling. This tree with its petals is a metaphor. What is the poet really describing?
   The "millions of petals" falling from the "invisible blossoming tree" are snowflakes falling.

2. If you did not know the title of the poem, which words would suggest that the "petals" are not really petals but snow?
   Suggestive words include "bitter and chill," "cool and white," "drifted" (reminiscent of *snowdrift*), as well as the fact that the tree is "invisible."

3. Identify five verbs that describe the action of the "petals":
   drifted, blew, lifted, flew, fell

4. Did you notice that the verbs in lines 8 and 9 rhyme? Identify the rhyming pairs.
   drifted / lifted   blew / flew

5. *Alliteration* is the use of words with the same or similar beginning sounds, as in "Peter Piper picked a peck of pickled peppers." Read aloud this line from "Snow Toward Evening" and notice the repeated *s* sound:

   > Grew intensely **s**oft and **s**till.

   Identify the alliteration in the last line of the poem. Read it aloud and underline the letter of the repeated sound:

   > <u>F</u>ell with the <u>f</u>alling night.
   > Tip: Note that the /f/ sound is echoed in the preceding two lines, though not always at the beginnings of the words: "Drifted and blew, / Lifted and flew...."

Activity

7. Rhyme Schemes

Students who have studied literature in the earlier grades of K12's Language Arts curriculum have already explored *rhyme scheme*. Depending on your student's familiarity with this concept, you may need only to briefly review it, or you may wish to pause and discuss it in more detail.

> Georgie Porgie, pudding and p<u>ie,</u>
> Kissed the girls and made them <u>cry</u>!
> When the boys came out to <u>play,</u>
> Georgie Porgie ran a<u>way</u>.

When identifying the patterns of rhyme, we use a letter of the alphabet to stand for each new rhyme. Thus, in the nursery rhyme above, we use **a** to mark the first rhyme (pie/cry); and **b** to mark the second rhyme (play/way), and so on. We would write the rhyme scheme as **a a b b**.

Have your student complete the Rhyme Schemes page.

Answers:
1. Rhyme scheme of "The Tide in the River": **a a b a a b**
2. Rhyme scheme of "Snow Toward Evening": **a a b b c c d e e d**

Lesson 4: Of Children on Rooftops, and Birds Big and Small

The first poem presents a vivid snapshot of a child where he probably should not be. The next two poems capture passing moments in the lives of two very different kinds of birds.

Objectives

Interpret poetry and support interpretations with evidence from the text.
Define and identify alliteration, simile, and personification.
Describe setting.
Identify action as conveyed through vivid verbs in poems.

Keywords

personification: giving human qualities to a thing or abstraction, for example: The kettle sang on the hearth.

setting: where and when a story takes place

simile: a figure of speech that compares two things, usually using the words *like* or *as,* for example, "like a thief in the night," "quiet as a mouse"

metaphor: a figure of speech that suggests or states a comparison between two unlike things, without using such words as *like* or *as,* for example: The cat's eyes were emeralds shining in the night.

Student Pages

Of Children on Rooftops, and Birds Big and Small
Close Reading (optional)

Materials

Classics for Young Readers, Vol. 5A, "Child on Top of a Greenhouse" (page 147), "The Eagle" (page 151), and "A Bird Came Down the Walk" (page 152)

First Reading: "Child on Top of a Greenhouse"

1. Get Ready

Vocabulary

Go over the vocabulary words with your student before he reads the poem.

billow: (n.) to rise in waves; to puff out or swell
When the wind *billowed* the sails, the sailboat began to speed through the water..

putty: (n.) a gooey mixture used to hold glass in window frames and fill cracks in wood
We put extra *putty* around the glass to help keep out the winter wind.

Think Ahead

Help your student anticipate the setting of the next poem by imagining a greenhouse, with walls and ceilings made of many glass panes, and many plants and flowers inside. You might ask him to close his eyes, picture a greenhouse, and tell you what he sees.

2. Read

Have your student read "Child on Top of a Greenhouse" once silently and a second time aloud. (You may want to read the poem aloud first.)

3. Discuss

1. The title tells you that the child is "on top of a greenhouse." What position is he in? Is he looking up or down? Find specific words in the poem that help you imagine exactly where the child is.

   The child is lying down on top of the greenhouse. He must be facing downward because the "seat of [his] britches" is up where it can be "billow[ed] out" by the wind. From his position, the child can see "half grown chrysanthemums staring up like accusers through the streaked glass"—if the mums are "staring up," then the child must be looking down at them.

2. Why do you think there are "splinters of glass and dried putty"?

   Accept any reasonable answer. Perhaps the child's foot has broken through one of the glass panes.

3. In line 3, the poet *personifies* the chrysanthemums. He gives the flowers human qualities: "the half-grown chrysanthemums staring up like accusers." What does this personification tell us about the speaker's state of mind?

   The personification suggests that the boy is feeling guilty about being on top of the greenhouse. If the flowers seem to be "accusing" him, then he must feel that he has done something wrong.

4. Many words in the poem express the action going on around the child, such as the wind "billowing" in the first line. Identify and list more of these "-ing" words that convey the action surrounding the boy: staring, flashing, rushing, plunging, tossing, pointing, shouting

   Tip: You might want to discuss how this poem works grammatically. It seems to be written as one long sentence, but there is no main verb. The action is conveyed through the various present participles (billowing, staring, flashing, etc.) in the poem. While there is a great deal of ongoing action, all of the action seems to be suspended in a single instant—there is no progress of events in the poem. It might be compared to the effect of a photograph, a moment captured in time.

5. The last line of the poem describes "everyone pointing up and shouting!" What do you think they might be saying?

   Accept any reasonable response, for example: "Get down from there! Be careful you might fall!"

Second Reading: "The Eagle"

4. Get Ready

Vocabulary
Go over the vocabulary words with your student before he reads the poem.

   crag: (n.) a rough, sharp, steep rock or cliff
   The mountain climber struggled to pull himself up the rocky *crag*.

azure: (n. or adj.) a sky-blue color
There was not a cloud to be seen as the sun shone brightly in the clear *azure* sky.

Think Ahead

This short poem is packed with descriptive and figurative language. Your student should review the terms *alliteration, simile,* and *personification* by matching them with their definitions.

1. alliteration   =   c. use of words with the same or similar beginning sounds
2. simile   =   a. a figure of speech that compares two things, using the words *like* or *as*
3. personification =   b. giving human qualities to a thing or abstraction

5. Read

Have your student read "The Eagle" once silently and a second time aloud. (You may want to read the poem aloud first.)

6. Discuss

1. Describe the *setting* of the poem. Where is this eagle?

    The eagle is high on a mountain, on a "crag . . . close to the sun" with the clear sky ('the azure world") above and around him, and the "wrinkled sea" below.

2. Identify the four verbs that tell what the eagle is doing and list them in the blanks below. What picture of the eagle is suggested by the first three verbs? How does the last verb change this picture?

    Line 1: he clasps
    Line 3: he stands
    Line 5: he watches
    Line 6: he falls

    The first three verbs paint a picture of the eagle in stillness, standing and watching (but still suggesting that he is full of an energy barely held in check and waiting to break loose). In the sixth line, the stillness turns to movement as "like a thunderbolt he falls."

3. How is the eagle personified in line 1?

    In line 1, the eagle is personified—given human qualities—when his talons are described as "crooked hands."

4. Identify the simile the poet uses to describe the eagle and write it here:

    like a thunderbolt he falls

    What two things does the simile compare? What does the simile tell you about the movement of the eagle?

    The simile compares the falling (the downward flight) of the eagle to a thunderbolt, that is, a bolt of lightning with the accompanying thunder. The simile tells us that the movement of the eagle is sudden, powerful, perhaps threatening as he flashes downward from the high cliff.

5. Read aloud the first line of the poem and listen for the alliteration. Underline the first letters of the words that have the same beginning sounds:

    He <u>c</u>lasps the <u>c</u>rag with <u>c</u>rooked hands.

Third Reading: "A Bird Came Down the Walk"

7. Get Ready

Vocabulary
Go over the vocabulary words with your student before he reads the poem.

> **convenient:** (adj.) handy; easy to get to or use; just right for the situation
> When I want to see a movie, I can walk to a *convenient* theater just two blocks from our apartment.

> **plash:** (v.) to splash
> My baby sister loves to *plash* around in the bathtub.

> **seam:** (n.) a line where two things (usually cloth) come together
> The *seam* of Margaret's shirt tore while she was climbing the ladder.

> **stir:** (v.) to move or cause to move slightly
> When a bee landed on my nose, I didn't *stir* at all, not even an eyelash, until it flew away.

Think Ahead
Go over the background information on Emily Dickinson: One of the greatest American poets, she was born in Amherst, Massachusetts, in 1830. She wrote her poems and tucked them away in boxes, or sent some to her friends. Only after her death were her poems collected and published in a book.

In her poems, Emily Dickinson had her own unusual way of capitalizing words, and she followed her own ideas about punctuation.

8. Read

Have your student read "A Bird Came Down the Walk" once silently and a second time aloud. (You may want to read the poem aloud first.)

9. Discuss

1. In line 2, the speaker says of the bird, "He did not know I saw." Imagine the scene in your mind. Where might the speaker be?
    > Accept any reasonable answer. For example, the speaker might be in a yard peeking out from behind a tree, or peering out a window.

2. Tell in your own words what the bird does in the first two stanzas of the poem. (Note: An "angleworm" is an earthworm.)
    > In the first stanza, the bird eats a worm; in the second stanza, the bird drinks water ("dew") and hops aside so that a beetle can get by.

3. Look at the language used to describe the bird in the first two stanzas. Some of it is odd and playful. For example, is there any other way for a bird to eat a worm than "raw"? When the bird drinks "a Dew from a convenient Grass," can you almost imagine him washing down his meal with a refreshing

beverage? And what does it suggest about the bird that he "hopped sideways . . . to let a Beetle pass"?

> Accept any reasonable answer. For example, when the bird hops sideways "to let a beetle pass," it suggests that he is a polite and courteous little creature.

4. Identify a simile in the third stanza, and explain what two things the simile is comparing.

> Simile: the bird's eyes look "like frightened Beads." The simile compares eyes to beads. (Notice, however, how the poet gives inanimate objects—beads—a human emotion, fear, when she describes them as "frightened" beads.)

5. In the fourth stanza, when the speaker offers the bird a crumb, the bird flies away. But the speaker doesn't say that the bird *flew* home. She says he "unrolled his feathers and rowed" home. The poet is using a surprising metaphor here. To what is the poet comparing the bird?

> She is comparing the bird to a boat—in particular, the metaphor compares the flight of the bird through the air to the way a boat travels on water (the "Ocean"). The bird "rowed" himself home through the "Ocean" of air.

Optional Activities

10. Close Reading

If your student would like to dig deeper into the last two stanzas of "A Bird Came Down the Walk," have him read the Close Reading page. You will want to read along with him and discuss the points of interpretation.

Tip: Emphasize that the goal of close reading is to help understand and appreciate the poem by paying attention to the language. The goal is *not* to translate the poetic language into plain factual language that tells "what the poem means." In many cases, there are many possible meanings. Your student should not be concerned about getting the "right" interpretation, but about letting his own imagination be challenged and stimulated by the poet's language.

11. Picture This

If your student would like to, have him draw or paint a picture that shows a particular moment in either "The Eagle" or "A Bird Came Down the Walk." He should first reread each poem, select one poem, and then pick a line or two from the poem to serve as a caption for his picture, for example:

> *He clasps the crag with crooked hands*
> > *or*
> *And then hopped sideways to the Wall*
> *To let a Beetle pass—*

Lesson 5: Unit Assessment: Passing Moments

Have your student complete the Unit 9 Assessment.

Objectives
Identify simile.
Identify metaphor.
Identify personification.
Identify alliteration.
Describe setting.
Identify rhyme scheme.
Interpret poetry and support interpretations with evidence from the text.

Materials
Classics for Young Readers, Vol. 5A

A. Figurative Language

1. metaphor
2. simile
3. personification
4. alliteration

B. Setting and Rhyme Scheme

5. Setting (time and place): It is a cold evening ("twilight) in February, near a snowy hill ("beside a hill / Smooth with new-laid snow")
6. Rhyme scheme: a b c b

C. Discuss a Poem

7. Answers will vary but should include a number of these points:
   - The speaker sends forth both the arrow and the song: he "shot" the arrow and "breathed" the song.
   - He did not know where either the song or the arrow went: he says of each, "It fell to earth, I knew not where."
   - Later ("long afterward"), he finds both. The arrow is "unbroke" in a tree. And the song he finds "in the heart of a friend."
   - The song might also be described as, like the arrow, "unbroke," since the speaker finds it "from beginning to end."

After your student completes the assessment, enter the results online.

Lesson 6: Semester Review

Check your student's recall and understanding, and prepare for the Semester Assessment with this review.

Objectives

Demonstrate comprehension of text.

Demonstrate knowledge of major characters, incidents, terms, or authors.

Identify characters from passages from the text.

Use facts and details from the story to discuss choices and consequences.

Make inferences and draw conclusions.

Identify the theme.

Interpret poetry and support interpretations with evidence from the text.

Identify the tone of a poem.

Distinguish between literal and figurative language.

Identify the setting.

Identify simile.

Identify metaphor.

Identify personification.

Identify alliteration.

Identify rhyme scheme.

Distinguish between fact and opinion.

Identify main idea and details.

Identify the author's purpose.

Compare and contrast information.

Student Pages

Semester Review

All About Genre

Materials

Classics for Young Readers, Vol. 5A

American Lives and Legends

Curious Creatures

Curious Creatures projects

crayons

scissors

1. Poetry Detective

Review skills by reading aloud or acting out and discussing some of this semester's poems and stories.

Have your student read aloud or act out one or more poems below. As necessary, review how to think about the speaker, decide how to say the lines, and choose movements or gestures appropriate to the action. Then have him rehearse the lines. He does not need to memorize them.

Poems:

"Spring"

"Winter the Huntsman"
"On a Snowy Day"
"The Leaves Do Not Mind at All"
"The Eagle"
"Snow Toward Evening"
"The Arrow and the Song"

For some students, speaking expressively is a challenge. Your student will enjoy and be inspired by hearing you model good, dramatic expressive speaking. Suggested discussion questions:

- How does the speaker feel during this part of the poem? How can you say your line to show how the speaker feels?
- What do you think the speaker's voice sounds like?
- How might the speaker move?

Provide encouragement and constructive criticism as your student rehearses. Encourage him to speak loudly and clearly. Sit at a distance from him, as though you were in the audience. Is he speaking loudly and clearly enough for you to understand him?

When he finishes, discuss the following questions to review some of the skills he has learned this semester.

- Describe the setting and tone of the poem.

    As necessary, remind your student that the *setting* is where and when the poem takes place. The *tone* is the attitude or emotion conveyed in speaking or writing. For example, the tone is happy, lively, and excited in the opening lines of Karla Kuskin's "Spring": "I'm shouting / I'm singing / I'm swinging through the trees." Compare that to the sad, gloomy tone in the opening lines of Judith Viorst's "Since Hanna Moved Away": "The tires on my bike are flat. / The sky is grouchy gray. / At least it sure feels like that / Since Hanna moved away."

- Give one example of literal language from the poem. If there isn't one, make up an example that could fit in the poem.

    Remind your student that literal language describes words used plainly and factually, for their exact, standard meaning.

- Find an example of figurative language. If there isn't one, make up an example that could fit in the poem.

    Remind your student that figurative language uses figures of speech, such as metaphor, simile, and personification, for poetic effect rather than for precise, factual meaning.

    Tip: As necessary, review with him that similes and metaphors are phrases that compare one thing to another. A simile is a figure of speech that compares two things, using the words *like* or *as,* for example: "quiet as a mouse." A metaphor is a figure of speech that suggests or states a comparison between two unlike things, without using the words *like* or *as,* for example: "The cat's eyes were emeralds shining in the night"; or, "The wind was a torrent of darkness among the gusty trees, The moon was a ghostly galleon tossed upon cloudy seas." (from "The Highwayman" by Alfred Noyes)

- Show where there is alliteration in the poem. If there is no alliteration, make up a line that alliterates that could fit in or after the poem.

    Remind your student that to alliterate means to start each main word in a phrase with the same sound, for example: **P**eter **P**iper **p**icked a **p**eck of **p**ickled **p**eppers.

- Use letters to write the poem's rhyme scheme.

    Remind your student that the *rhyme scheme* is the pattern of rhymes in a poem. Note that she should use a letter of the alphabet to stand for each new rhyme. Thus, we use *a* to mark the first rhyme, *b* to mark the second rhyme, and so on.

2. Author's Purpose

Review author's purpose, nonfiction, and poetry skills by discussing *Curious Creatures* articles and projects and reflecting on the work of two poets from the Early American Lives unit.

Have your student review the projects he completed during the *Curious Creatures* unit. Brainstorm with him a list of ways an author can present nonfiction information, which may include some of the suggestions below. When he finishes, have him write four ways on the lines provided on the Student Guide.

magazine article	brochure
travel guide	instruction booklet
time line	story
encyclopedia article	newspaper article or news report

Have your student review the introductions to "Eating Like a Bird," "Stormflight," and "Lingering Leeches." Then discuss the following questions about hooks and audience.

- Describe each hook. Does it ask a question, tell a story, or present the information as if the reader were there?

    The hook in "Eating Like a Bird" asks a question and presents the reader with a familiar phrase, the hook in "Stormflight" presents information as if the reader were there, and the hook in "Lingering Leeches" begins with an anecdote.

- Authors use hooks to catch a reader's attention and to give information about the main idea. Choose one article from the *Curious Creatures* unit. Describe the hook, then give the main idea of the article. What does the hook tell you about the main idea?

    Accept any reasonable response. Remind your student that the *main idea* is the author's most important point. Ask him to look over the article, think about the title, and identify the author's most important point. Then discuss the information the hook gives about the main idea, for example:
    - In "Eating Like a Bird," the hook is a familiar saying that is the *opposite* of how birds eat.
    - In "The Ocean's Cleaning Stations," the hook tells a story that describes how the cleaning stations work.
    - In "Stormflight," the hook describes the sensations that would accompany watching a termite migration.
    - In "A Mom with a Mission," the hook is a statement that is the *opposite* of how treehopper moms behave.

- In "Lingering Leeches," the hook shows two different perspectives on leeches.

Discuss how poetry is another way to share information, fiction *or* nonfiction. Remind your student that Henry Wadsworth Longfellow and Phillis Wheatley both wrote poems that provided nonfiction information. As necessary, review these poems on pages 13 and 21 of *American Lives and Legends.* Then have your student write a poem about his favorite subject from the *Curious Creatures* unit. The poem does not have to rhyme, but should include two or more facts from the article and one or more examples of figurative language.

Tip: If your student has difficulty, have him write three interesting or unusual facts about the subject. Then encourage him to use the facts to help him think of something he could compare the subject to, for example: diving bird – jet pilot or falling star, cleaner fish – a person doing "living" laundry, termites – a cloud, treehoppers – knights, leeches – slimy trains.

Example poem:
Knight of the Thorn
She is a knight in shining armor!
Her pronotum is her helmet,
her legs are her lances.
Bravely she defends her children
from dragon-lizards of the forest.
Treehopper mom, fight bravely!
So your children can grow up
To also be knights someday.

3. All About Genre

Remind your student that he studied different genres this semester. A genre is a category of literature. During the semester, your student read different kinds of fiction and nonfiction, including biographies, autobiographies, legends, hero tales, short stories, and narrative poetry. Some of these genres share characteristics. Have your student review the genres of legend, hero tale, autobiography, and narrative poem by completing the All About Genre chart. He may use his books, responses in his Reading Notebook, and projects to help him answer the questions.

As necessary, review the following descriptions with your student:
- A *legend* is a story that has been handed down from the past. It may include historical characters and facts, but the story has changed over time and become fiction.
- A *hero tale* is a story in which the main character battles an enemy that seems much stronger and almost impossible to defeat. But, in the end, he or she triumphs against all odds.
- An *autobiography* is the life story of a person written by that person. It is nonfiction. It contains facts, information, and the feelings and thoughts of the author.
- A *biography* is the story of a person's life.

Answers:
Legend
handed down from the past
includes historical events or characters

includes fictional events
Examples: "The Legend of Sleepy Hollow," "Rip Van Winkle"

Hero Tale
handed down from the past
main character defeats a terrible enemy
includes fictional events
Examples: "The Story of Mulan," "St. George and the Dragon"

Autobiography
includes historical events or characters
includes facts and information
tells the story of a person's life
is about the author
Examples: Excerpt in "Young Benjamin Franklin"

Biography
includes historical events or characters
includes facts and information
tells the story of a person's life
Examples: "Young Benjamin Franklin," "Phillis Wheatley"

4. Name That Character!

Have your student match characters with their stories and authors, and briefly summarize each plot.

1.   "Oh, he would sit on a wet rock and fish all day even if he didn't get a single nibble. He would carry a fowling-piece on his shoulder for hours, trudging through woods and swamps, up hill and down dale, to shoot a few squirrels or wild pigeons. And he would never refuse to help a neighbor. But as to doing his family duty, and keeping his farm in order, he found it impossible. In a word, he was ready to attend to everybody's business except his own."

   The character is Rip Van Winkle from "Rip Van Winkle," by Washington Irving. Sample summary: Rip Van Winkle follows a strange man up into the mountains, drinks from the flagon, and falls asleep. When he wakes up, he goes back into town and finds that twenty years have passed.

2.   "So the Prince had a special saddle made for it—very long it was—and one hundred and fifty seats were fitted to this. Its greatest pleasure was now to give pleasure to others, and it delighted in taking parties of children to the seaside. It flew through the air quite easily with its hundred and fifty little passengers, and would lie on the sand patiently waiting till they were ready to return. The children were very fond of it and used to call it 'dear,' a word which never failed to bring tears of affection and gratitude to its eyes."

   The character is the dragon from "The Last of the Dragons," by E. Nesbit. Sample summary: A princess and a prince make friends with the last of dragons instead of killing it. At the end of the story, the dragon becomes an airplane.

3.   "His head was small, and flat at top, with huge ears, and large green glassy eyes. He had a long snipe nose. It looked like a weathercock perched upon his skinny neck to tell which way the wind

blew. To see him striding over a hill on a windy day, with his clothes bagging and fluttering about him, one might have mistaken him for a scarecrow escaping from a cornfield."

> The character is Ichabod Crane from "The Legend of Sleepy Hollow," by Washington Irving.
> Sample summary: Ichabod Crane is a schoolteacher who tries to win Katrina von Tassel's heart. Brom Bones dresses up as the Headless Horseman and scares Ichabod. At the end of the story, it isn't clear whether Ichabod dies or goes away to live somewhere else.

4.   "He often read the priest's old books and got him to explain them. His dreamings and readings changed him. His dream-people were so fine that he began to feel sad about his shabby clothing, and to wish to be clean and better clothed.

   By and by, he began to act like a prince. His speech and manners became ceremonious and courtly. In time, the other boys of Offal Court looked up to him with a wondering awe. He seemed to know so much! And he could do and say such marvelous things!"

> The character is Tom Canty from "The Prince and the Pauper," by Mark Twain. Sample summary: A poor boy and a prince trade places. They learn much about each other's lives, and trade back right before Tom is crowned the King of England.

Tip: Your student may enjoy completing this activity as a game in which you read the quote aloud and give him a reasonable period of time to find the answer. If he answers correctly on the first try in the time allotted, award him five points; on the second try, three points; and on the third try, one point. You may wish to offer him small rewards or prizes for certain numbers of points.

5. Real Life Heroes

Have your student review, read aloud, or act out two of the selections from the Early American Lives unit. When he finishes, have him do the following things:

- Tell three important facts from each story.
  Remind your student that a *fact* is something that can be proven true. If you wish, have him find a fictional event in the story, as well.

- Describe an important choice each person made, why he or she made it, and the consequences of the choice.
  As necessary, have your student read aloud the part of the story in which the character made the choice.

- Explain one way the characters are alike and one way they are different.
  Encourage your student to compare the characters' positive qualities or their contributions. For example, Paul Revere and Sequoyah were both *determined*, while Sybil Ludington and Phillis Wheatley showed that people of all genders, races, and ages are capable of accomplishing great ends.

- Give an opinion about each person. What advice do you think each person might give people today?
  Review with your student the difference between fact and opinion. A *fact* is a statement that can be proven true, while an *opinion* is what a person feels or thinks about something. Opinions are not true or false. People can have different opinions about the same thing without being right or wrong.

6. Conflict, Resolution, and Theme

Review with your student that a *conflict* is a clash or struggle between people, ideas, or feelings. A character can have a conflict with the following:

- Another character or group of characters

  For example, in "Fire on the Mountain," Arha has a conflict with Haptom.

- His or her own thoughts and feelings

  For example, in "The Story of Mulan," Mulan experiences a conflict in her own feelings when she reaches the army camp. She feels sad and homesick, but she also wants to be strong and brave.

- His or her society or the natural world

  For example, in "Daniel in the Lion's Den," Daniel faces a conflict between his beliefs and the king's new law.

Have your student choose two characters from the list below and describe the conflict each character faces and how he or she resolves it.

- The king in "Salt and Bread"
- Ali in "Ali and the Magic Stew"
- Damocles in "The Sword of Damocles"
- Mulan in "The Story of Mulan"
- St. George or the princess in "St. George and the Dragon"
- Tom Canty in "The Prince and the Pauper"
- Ruth in "The Story of Ruth"
- David in "The Story of David"
- Daniel in "The Story of Daniel"

Tip: You may wish to review with your student that some characters face more than one conflict. For example, Ali experiences a conflict in his own feelings because he does not want to beg, but he wants to save his father's life. Then he has a conflict with those from whom he is trying to beg.

Next, review with your student that the *theme* of a story is the author's message. Discuss the following questions about theme with respect to the two stories your student chose. As necessary, remind your student that there may be more than one theme in a story.

- Describe each character at the beginning and end of the story. How does the character change?
- What do you think the character learns? Do you think the character would behave differently in the future? Why or why not?
- What do you think a reader can learn from the character's actions? What do you think the author wants readers to think about after reading the story?
- Look back to the list. Do any of the other stories have a theme that is similar to the story you chose?

  If your student has difficulty, have him look for similar conflicts or examples of courage, compassion, humility, or fairness in the stories.

7. Optional: Lights, Camera, Action!

Prepare your student to rewrite a selection from a story as a scene from a play. First, have him choose an important moment in his favorite story to rewrite. As necessary, discuss with him the parts of a script, and have him look back to "The Prince and the Pauper" play on pages 93-108 in *Classics for Young Readers* for an example. Encourage him to make a list of characters in the story he chose, describe the setting, and include stage directions. Suggested discussion questions:

- Name the characters who appear in this scene.
- How does each character feel at the beginning of the scene? How does each character feel at the end of the scene? What words or phrases can you use to describe those feelings as stage directions?
- How might each character move or gesture as he or she speaks? Would one character move closer to another, or farther away? Why?
- Where does the scene take place? What props or scenery do you think the scene requires?

Guide him to use the characters' words as dialogue and rewrite their actions as stage directions. When he finishes, discuss the following questions about character and theme:

- Describe the important choice a character makes. Why do you think the character makes that choice?
- What words describe the character? Why?
- What can you learn from the character? Can you think of other stories in this unit that have a similar message?

    As necessary, remind your student that a *theme* is the author's message or "big idea." There can be more than one theme in a story.

Lesson 7: Semester Assessment

Check your student's recall and understanding with the Semester Assessment.

Lesson Notes

Make sure your student understands the directions for the Semester Assessment, then have him complete the assessment on his own. (He should not refer to the *Classics for Young Readers* book while doing Parts 1-4, but he may use his book for Part 5, the essay section.)

Objectives

Demonstrate comprehension of text.

Demonstrate knowledge of major characters, incidents, terms, or authors.

Use facts and details from the story to discuss choices and consequences.

Make inferences and draw conclusions.

Identify the theme.

Identify the tone of a poem.

Identify the setting.

Distinguish between literal and figurative language.

Identify the rhyme scheme.

Distinguish between fact and opinion.

Identify main idea and details.

Identify the author's purpose.

Compare and contrast characters.

Materials

Classics for Young Readers, Volume 5A

Part 1: Genre

Answers:

1. c
2. d
3. a
4. b

Part 2: Names and Faces

Answers:

5. d
6. b
7. b
8. c
9. a

Part 3: Poetry

Answers:

10. b
11. a
12. Rhyme scheme:

    a

    b

    c

    b

    d

    e

    f

    e

13. Accept any reasonable answer, for example: The tone of the poem is rough and energetic. Words like *gusty* and *dashing* make me think of things rushing and crashing roughly and with lots of energy. Also, the fog's skirts are *torn,* and clothes tear when you're running too fast and get them caught on something.

Part 4: Reading Comprehension

14. c
15. d
16. a and b
17. c
18. Accept any reasonable answer, for example: For the hook, the author used a surprising fact. He asked the reader to think of as many things as possible that use electricity in ten seconds. Then he said that most people who lived in the early 1800s couldn't have thought of more than two things in ten minutes.
19. Accept any reasonable answer, for example: In the hook, the author showed that in the early 1800s, people did not have many uses for electricity.
20. Accept any reasonable answer, for example: The telegraph changed the way people thought about electricity because it showed them that they could use electricity to do useful work.
21. a

Part 5: Writing

22. Your student should write an essay of five paragraphs comparing and contrasting characters' choices and themes from two stories. Have him choose one pair of characters from the list and follow the outline given in the Semester Assessment. As necessary, he may refer his *Classics for Young Readers* book to plan and write his essay.

Test Readiness

Test Readiness

Test Ready: Reading Longer Passages

Many of K12's Grade 5 Literature lessons help develop your student's reading comprehension skills. To complement those lessons, we also provide a test preparation booklet from Curriculum Associates called *Test Ready: Reading Longer Passages.* This booklet serves a specific practical purpose: its content and format—reading selections followed by multiple-choice questions and a short writing exercise—help prepare your student for similar exercises on many standardized tests.

About Test Readiness

- The Lessons in *Test Ready: Reading Longer Passages* provide practice in answering reading comprehension questions similar to those found on standardized tests.

- The test preparation booklet includes reading selections, referred to as passages, from the following genres: Folktales, Narratives, Myths, Informational Text, and Biographies. (Note: K12's recommended schedule includes most, but not all, of the lessons in the Test Ready booklet.)

- The Answer Form on the back cover of the student booklet gives your student the opportunity to record his answers in a "fill-in-the-bubble" format similar to many standardized tests.

- The Practice Test at the back of the booklet gives your student the opportunity to practice answering multiple-choice questions and writing to a prompt. In the recommended Language Arts schedule, you guide your student through this test as his first experience with the Test Ready materials.

Introducing Your Student to Test Readiness

- Read and have your student read all of the information on the inside cover of the *Test Ready: Reading Longer Passages* booklet. Discuss the information with him. Pay particular attention to the testing tips. Encourage your student to refer to these tips as he completes the lessons.

- Explain that the booklet contains readings, called passages, of varying types. Each lesson has two parts: Part One is a series of multiple-choice questions, and Part Two is a writing exercise.

- Have your student turn to the Answer Form. Advise him to use the form provided to answer the multiple-choice questions in his booklet. You may wish to have him tear the Answer Form from his booklet at this time.

- If your student is unfamiliar with an answer form, practice by calling out a number and letter (for example, number 10, answer C) and having him point to the corresponding bubble. It may also help to have him place an index card or piece of paper as a marker under a line when he is working. If he has difficulty using the form, have him mark the answers in his booklet. When he has completed the lesson, help him transfer his answers to the answer form.

- Look at the illustrations that accompany the passages. Remind your student to look at the pictures and read any titles or accompanying text when completing a lesson.

Lesson Scheduling and Procedures

Lessons are divided into two parts and serve as preparation for two types of testing. In Part One, your student practices answering comprehension questions. In Part Two, he writes in response to a prompt, as required in many standardized tests. In the recommended Language Arts schedule, your student completes Part One and Part Two during one session.

Be sure to read the section below on "The First Session: Start with the Practice Test."

Part One

Have your student read each passage silently and complete the multiple-choice questions that follow.

According to your student's experience with standardized testing, he may work though the exercises independently, or you may assist him until he is comfortable working on his own. The purpose of the program is to familiarize him with the testing format, and if he needs your guidance for a while, that's fine.

Part Two

Read the directions for the writing activity. Discuss the points that should be included in his response. Remind him to include details from the passage to support his response. Have him draft his response on scrap paper and then write his final copy in the booklet.

After he has completed the writing activity, use the remaining time to review his response and if needed, discuss ways he might improve his answer. See the note in "Correction and Scoring Procedures" concerning the use of the Short Answer Checklist.

The First Session: Start with the Practice Test

In the first session, you will guide your student through the Practice Test at the back of *Test Ready Plus: Reading.*

- If he has not already done so, have your student remove the Answer Form from the booklet.

- Turn to the Practice Test.

- Point out the "Go on to the next page" and "STOP" symbols in the lower right-hand corner of the pages. Instruct your student to follow those directions when he reaches them in the workbook.

- Note that the symbols indicate that he is to work straight through Part One of the Practice Test.

- Work through the Practice Test together. First, read the sentences above the title. Then have your student read the selection silently. If he has difficulty and asks for help, have him read the passage aloud. Encourage him to attempt pronunciation of difficult words, and if he becomes frustrated, tell him to simply pronounce the word as he thinks it should be said.

- Complete items 1-15. Instruct your student to read each item and *all* of the responses before he selects his answer. If he is unsure about an answer, have him look back to the passage. It may also be helpful to have him first read all the items, then go back and reread the passage. You may proceed through the booklet together, or have him to work through several items on his own and then check back with you. Periodically check to see that he is answering each item in the correctly numbered row on the Answer Form.

- If your student has been working independently, take time to review and discuss his answers before he begins Part Two.

- Read and discuss the directions for Part Two. Remind your student to use details from the story to support his answer. Have him draft his response on scrap paper and then write his final copy in the booklet.

Correction and Scoring Procedures

The Answer Key and the Short Answer Checklist may be found at the end of this section. Be sure to keep them readily available because you will need to use them frequently.

Part One
If your student is working independently, allow about 15-20 minutes after he has completed the reading and questions to review and discuss his answers. Encourage him to explain some of his responses. Review any incorrect answers and help him understand why the answer choice was incorrect. Reading aloud the part of the passage that corresponds to the incorrect answer can often clear up misconceptions.

Part Two
A Short Answer Checklist is provided. Evaluate your student's response by answering *yes* or *no* to the four questions. Assign one point for each *yes* response. Discuss ways your student can improve his response.

Test Readiness Short Answer Checklist

	Yes	No
Responds to or addresses the question or prompt	☐	☐
Sticks to the topic	☐	☐
Is organized and clear	☐	☐
There are 4 errors or less in grammar, spelling, and punctuation	☐	☐

Test Readiness

Test Ready: Reading Longer Passages Answer Key

Refer to this page for answers to all of the assessment questions. Be sure to keep this answer key readily available because you will need to use it frequently.

Lesson 1	Lesson 2	Lesson 3	Lesson 4
1. d	1. c	1. d	1. b
2. d	2. b	2. b	2. a
3. c	3. b	3. d	3. d
4. b	4. c	4. c	4. c
5. d	5. d	5. c	5. b
6. b	6. d	6. b	6. d
7. d	7. c	7. b	7. b
8. c	8. c	8. c	8. c
9. c	9. a	9. b	9. d
10. d	10. b	10. c	10. d
11. b	11. a	11. a	11. a
12. b	12. b	12. b	12. b
13. a	13. d	13. b	13. d
14. b	14. b	14. b	14. c
15. d	15. c	15. d	15. d

Lesson 5	Lesson 6	Practice Test
1. d	1. b	1. b
2. c	2. c	2. b
3. d	3. b	3. a
4. a	4. b	4. d
5. d	5. c	5. c
6. d	6. a	6. d
7. c	7. b	7. c
8. b	8. c	8. c
9. b	9. b	9. b
10. d	10. c	10. c
11. b	11. d	11. a
12. c	12. b	12. d
13. a	13. b	13. d
14. b	14. b	14. b
15. c	15. c	15. c